BIOGRAPHY OF THE DOLLAR

BIOGRAPHY
OF THE
DOLLAR

HOW THE MIGHTY BUCK CONQUERED
THE WORLD AND WHY IT'S UNDER SIEGE

CRAIG KARMIN

CROWN
BUSINESS
NEW YORK

Published in the United States by Crown Business, an imprint of the Crown
Publishing Group, a division of Random House, Inc., New York.
www.crownpublishing.com

Crown Business is a trademark and the Rising Sun colophon is a
registered trademark of Random House, Inc.

Library of Congress Cataloging-in-Publication Data
Karmin, Craig.
Biography of the dollar: how the mighty buck conquered the world
and why it's under siege / Craig Karmin.
1. Dollar, American.   2. Foreign exchange.   3. International finance.   I.
Title.
HG540.K37 2008
332.4'973—dc22   2007035501

ISBN 978-0-307-33986-7

Printed in the United States of America

Design by Lenny Henderson

10   9   8   7   6   5   4   3   2   1

First Edition

For Susanne

CONTENTS

Introduction

One dark November day, people in the Netherlands turned on their TVs to watch something few thought they'd ever see: The mighty dollar was collapsing before their eyes.

The currency's sudden demise begins at 1:00 A.M. Greenwich mean time (GMT), when a trader at a large Singapore bank receives a big order to sell dollars. Rumors spread quickly that the request came from a giant hedge fund that needs to unload its dollar-denominated assets at any cost. Central banks in Japan, South Korea, and China—all big-dollar holders—start buying more dollars to steady the greenback's decline. But by now panic has set in, and the central banks' dollar purchases are overwhelmed by private investors, traders, and speculators who are scrambling to sell dollars as fast as they can.

The dollar is sinking rapidly when trading opens in Europe. The region's bond markets have frozen up and its stock markets all plunge more than 10 percent in a few scary minutes. Even before the European Central Bank (ECB) announces that it will provide emergency loans to commercial banks, the ECB's phone lines are jammed with desperate calls. Traders report that the dollar's unforeseen collapse has put countless hedge funds out of business. A Dutch news anchor reports winding lines at ATMs in Amsterdam, where crowds turn hostile after finding the machines empty. The city's foreign exchange kiosks shut their doors. At 1:00 P.M. GMT, a mere twelve hours after the crisis started with that big trade in Singapore, Banca di Torino becomes the first European bank to go under.

Then trading begins in the United States. The dollar keeps falling. A dispute breaks out between America's Federal Reserve and the European Central Bank over how best to respond. The ECB wants to enforce a new fixed exchange rate between the euro and the dollar, but the Fed balks. It decides instead to freeze all trans-Atlantic financial transactions. The United Kingdom sides with Washington, threatening to quit the European Union unless the ECB backs down. But the oil producing nations of OPEC ally with Europe, announcing that crude oil prices will now be priced in euros instead of dollars. Back in Amsterdam, at the end of this dizzying day, a man calls for a taxi to take him to a train station. With both the dollar and the euro in flux, he pays the driver with three packs of Marlboro cigarettes.

This scenario, of course, did not happen in the real world. But it did play out on a Dutch television network in 2005. Reminiscent of Orson Welles's famous *War of the Worlds* radio hoax, many viewers who tuned in mid-program and saw real-life news anchors reporting the dollar's meltdown believed the fictional account to be terrifyingly real. Some even raced to withdraw cash from their ATMs before it was too late. "We wanted to show that the world is a more dangerous place financially than most people realize," Maarten Schinkel, a Dutch economics newspaper reporter who wrote the script for this film, told me. "What people don't understand is how much the world is still dependent on the dollar."

Financial Armageddon, if it ever comes, probably won't unfold as quickly or dramatically as Schinkel depicts. But he's right that the dollar's presence has become so ubiquitous in our world that it is like water to a fish. It's around us every day, and we take for granted that it always will be. Few of us ever pause to consider how powerful a force the dollar is in the world today and the degree to which it drives both America's and the globe's prosperity. Likewise, few reflect on the possibility that the dollar's privileged status might one day end. And what that would mean for us all.

This book aims to shed a bit of light on these issues with a scenic tour of the dollar through the global economy. It examines the greenback's allure, its history, its many functions, and its role as a catalyst for globalization. These pages also assert that the dollar's emergence as the world's main currency is driving two of the defining trends in the world economy today.

The first development is unambiguously positive: The dollar's universal acceptance has been an essential force behind the world's powerful economic expansion. This has swollen the ranks of the middle class and lifted many others from poverty. But the flipside has been cause for concern: Enduring demand for the dollar has also encouraged the United States to run up enormous—some would say unsustainable—foreign debts and record trade deficits. The United States now pays out the equivalent of $1 million each day for every man, woman, and child in the country—just in interest payments on that foreign debt. Washington's ability to assuage international borrowers, who are becoming increasingly fearful these debts and deficits are running out of control, may well determine how long the dollar can continue to enjoy its special status. And as we will see, loss of that status would have serious consequences for Americans and the rest of the world alike.

To understand why any change in the dollar's global role would have such a far-reaching effect, it helps to appreciate how almighty the buck really is. Even by the standards of a military and economic superpower, the dollar's supremacy has been remarkable. While the U.S. economy accounts for about 30 percent of global gross domestic product and American companies compose nearly 50 percent of the world stock market capitalization, the dollar's dominance is greater still. It figures in nearly 90 percent of all trades in the more than $3.2-trillion-a-day foreign exchange market. Nearly two-thirds of the world's central bank reserves are held in dollars.

In the post World War II era, the dollar has become the primary unit of international trade and finance. Emerging market nations borrow in it. China pegs its currency to it to ensure stability. All major commodities, from oil to soybeans, are priced in dollars. The dollar is truly the world's currency in that of the $760 billion in circulation, about two-thirds are held abroad. Foreigners collect and spend these dollars even though, since the United States abandoned the gold standard in 1971, they are now backed by nothing more than faith in America.

"The dollar is the greatest monetary achievement in the history of the world," says James Grant, a financial historian and publisher of *Grant's Interest Rate Observer*. "It is a paper claim of no inherent value that is accepted on its face in every corner of the earth. There is nothing behind it but the idea of America."

So inescapable is the dollar's reach that even the nation's historic adversaries have embraced it. Julia Kiraly, an economic consultant I met at Café Gerbeaud in Budapest, recalls that during the Cold War, Hungarians were allowed a trip abroad every three years. Her priority during each visit to western Europe in the 1970s and 1980s was to bring back as many dollars as she could hide in her apartment. Even when the Cold War ended and she was living in Belgium in the mid-1990s, Kiraly would continue to convert her Belgian franc paychecks into dollars. "I knew it didn't make any sense," she said, explaining that all her expenses were in the Belgian currency. "But I am from the generation where we weren't comfortable unless we had a big deposit in U.S. dollars."

In the other capitals of the Eastern bloc, a sort of "dollar apartheid" flourished in the early 1990s, as demand for the currency pushed it out from the shadows of the black markets. A visitor to Moscow in the middle of that decade would find that rubles were fine for buying toilet paper at the corner store or purchasing a ticket for the metro. But the prices at the city's nouvelle French restaurants and the cover charge at trendy nightspots were settled in dollars. And while Saddam Hussein, in an act of rebellion against the United States, used to insist on being paid in euros for Iraqi oil, his captors found in his possession $750,000, all in neat stacks of one hundred dollar bills. There was not a euro among them.

Anti-American protesters might torch the Stars and

Stripes or throw a brick through the window of a local McDonald's, but when was the last time you saw footage of anyone burning that cotton-and-linen rectangle bearing the visage of Benjamin Franklin? Forget Coca-Cola, Microsoft, Toyota, Manchester United, the Christian cross, or the Islamic scimitar—the most powerful, most well-recognized, and most widely used and distributed symbol on earth is arguably $.

Yet, at the start of the new millennium, it is hard to mistake signs that the dollar's unrivaled supremacy is in the early stages of inevitable decline. The first sign is the birth of the euro in 1999, now the currency of thirteen European nations—more than 317 million people—and soon perhaps several more. "For the first time there is the prospect of another currency to rival the dollar," says Barry Eichengreen, an international economist at the University of California, Berkeley, who has written extensively on currencies. "The euro has permanently changed the international financial landscape. The question is how quickly the transition will go."

By most accounts, any transition will be gradual. Global markets and central banks don't readily switch reserve currencies. The pound sterling remained the world standard for some forty years after the United States had eclipsed Britain as the world's economic superpower. Moreover, few see the dollar being completely knocked off the mountaintop—at least by the euro, and not for a while. Rather, economists see the euro, and eventually the Chinese yuan, playing increasingly important roles in the global economy, chipping away at the dollar's dominance.

Some of this is already under way. Central banks from Moscow to Riyadh have diversified their reserves to include more euros. While this shift in part may reflect concern over a dollar bear market that started around 2002 and has wiped away more than half of the dollar's value against the euro, the rise of a viable alternative currency suggests central banks will store a portion of their reserves in euros on a permanent basis. Washington can slow this transition by cutting deficits and enacting measures to encourage private savings, steps that would likely help the dollar rally and raise its value. But U.S. policymakers cannot change the broader dynamics that lead central banks to diversify their holdings.

The financial crisis of 1997 and 1998 also marked a shift. Following a depletion of their dollar reserves, most Asian and Latin American countries stopped pegging their currencies to the dollar, allowing their currencies instead to float more freely. As governments also whipped their economies into shape, paying down their debt and building up their reserves, they found that they could borrow money through the international markets in their own currencies. Global investors no longer insist that these bond transactions be sold in dollars.

The growing sophistication of financial systems could diminish the dollar's central role in foreign exchange trading, too. One reason the dollar figures in 90 percent of all activity is because it serves as a go-between when transactions are made between more thinly traded currencies, say the Colombian peso for the Thai baht. But superior technology is expected one day to allow these currencies to swap directly, rather than into dollars first, thus further eroding at the margins the dollar's central role in global finance.

For now, however, the dollar remains the name of

the game in currency trading. So we'll start the dollar tour in America's financial capital, New York City, at the midtown Manhattan office of hedge fund managers FX Concepts. The firm is among the most active currency speculators in the world, turning over as much as $3 billion a day in currency trades. In Chapter 1, you'll meet John Taylor, the sixty-four-year-old cofounder of FX Concepts and a pioneer in the field of foreign exchange trading. Taylor offers a ringside seat at the frenetic world of currency trading, where the dollar's value is determined each day and individual fortunes can be made or lost. You'll witness the ways big hedge fund traders decide whether to bet on the dollar's rise or its fall and how a small number of people have come to have such a disproportionate effect on your currency's value.

In Chapter 2, we'll travel to the Bureau of Engraving and Printing (BEP) in Washington, D.C., where this arm of the U.S. Treasury Department cranks out 9 billion currency notes annually. The BEP is also in the advanced stages of its most important project: the newly designed $100 bill. Planned for a 2008 release, the new hundred is said to use the most sophisticated anti-counterfeit technology ever seen. It had better. The new bills must not only frustrate the growing army of at-home counterfeiters, with their powerful PCs and high-resolution color printers, they must foil the shadowy counterfeiters behind the extraordinary Supernotes—fakes so realistic they fool even most experts and have already undermined the dollar's acceptance in certain corners of the globe. Larry Felix, the new head of the BEP, takes you behind locked doors to show you how ink and paper merge to become dollars and to offer you a glimpse at what the government has planned to derail the funny money makers.

Chapter 3 takes us back in time to trace the rise of the dollar from its humble beginnings during the Civil War to its role as nexus of the global economy and as one of America's most potent symbols of power and influence. Along the way, you'll be introduced to Paul Warburg, the German-born banker most responsible for overcoming America's historic prejudice against central banks. He devised the Federal Reserve system, which proved to be the final piece in the puzzle for making the dollar an international currency. You'll also meet Paul Volcker, a towering figure of six foot seven who as Treasury undersecretary helped prod the United States to end the gold standard, releasing the dollar from a leash that had kept both U.S. and world economic growth from reaching their full potential. Years later, as Fed chairman, Volcker's series of interest rate increases would send the United States into recession to save the dollar's privileged status. That rescue would help set the stage for even greater economic growth in the final years of the twentieth century.

Next up, in Chapter 4, we visit South America, arriving at the poor, divided nation of Ecuador. Improbable as it may seem, it is here that one of the grand financial experiments of our time is unfolding. In 2000, after suffering years of massive devaluations and spiraling inflation, Ecuador scrapped its own currency, the sucre, for the U.S. dollar. Unlike other countries that peg their currencies directly to the dollar, or even countries that use the dollar alongside their own currency, Ecuador took a more drastic step. It eliminated the sucre entirely, throwing its lot in with the dollar in a desperate Hail Mary attempt to solve Ecuador's recurring economic problems. In this brave new world of dollarization, even the U.S. government was powerless to stop it. You'll hear from the country's winners, losers, and those who still aren't sure to which camp they belong: the central banker, the energy minister, middle-class yuppies, a Kia car dealer, a floral exporter, gardeners, a retired pensioner, housewives, and a college dean, among others. Together, they paint a complex portrait of the unique opportunities and unforeseen traps that await a nation that has sacrificed its currency to that of the world's lone superpower.

From Latin America, we'll travel to Asia in Chapter 5 for a stop at the corridors of financial power in Seoul, South Korea. The country's massive build-up of dollar reserves in recent years has had an unexpected side-effect: Investor fears that the Koreans might one day sell down their dollar holdings has changed the nature of the relationship between South Korea and the United States. In today's interconnected global economy, the value of America's currency sits, to some degree, with people like Heung-Sik Choo, a mild-mannered official at South Korea's central bank. His decisions, along with those of his counterpart Keehong Rhee at a special government fund set up to manage the country's reserves more aggressively, have the potential to rock the dollar. You'll learn a bit more about their current thinking and the investment process embraced by Asian central banks with big-dollar holdings that increasingly hold the fate of the dollar in their hands.

The dollar tour ends back in the American heartland,

St. Louis, Missouri, for Chapter 6. That's where Chuck Butler, president of EverBank, is sowing a radical idea among millions of his countrymen: The dollar is not the only game in town anymore. He spends his days warning people to protect themselves from its inevitable decline. His solution is a foreign-currency savings account or certificate of deposit from EverBank. Butler argues that the yawning U.S. deficits and bloated foreign debt levels will eventually force the dollar's value much lower. We'll look at how the end of the gold standard that freed the dollar to fuel the world's economic expansion also gave rise to these debts and deficits that have thrown the global economy into imbalance. That's raised the prospect that too many dollars may be circulating the planet and could be setting the greenback up for a big fall. With the equivalent of about $1 billion in EverBank's foreign-currency products, Butler is testimony that many middle-class people in the United States share some of his concern.

And well they should. Americans probably won't realize how good they had it under the dollar's reign until the day that reign is over. French president Charles de Gaulle once complained bitterly that the dollar's central role accorded the United States an "exorbitant privilege." Those hundreds of billions of dollars held abroad represent an interest-free loan to the U.S. government. America faces no foreign exchange costs when buying commodities as long as they are priced in dollars. Its businesses face little currency risk abroad because most of their transactions are also conducted in dollars.

"No other country in the world can run deficits as large as we have without having to tighten fiscal and monetary policy," says Benjamin Cohen, professor of international political economy at the University of California, Santa Barbara. Even average Americans enjoy this "exorbitant privilege" through lower interest rates on home and car loans that are made possible by the low interest rates the dollar can enjoy while still attracting foreign capital.

For how much longer, though? Whatever happens next, the dollar's grip on the world appears to be slowly loosening. You can see it for yourself. Russian law now prohibits restaurants, clubs, or merchants from listing their prices in dollars. I found in Hungary that store owners can tell you right away how much something costs in euros, but many are unaware these days of even the dollar exchange rate. Black market money-changers in Seoul say people now request Chinese yuan as often as they do dollars.

People abroad may consider that a welcome change after so many years under the dollar's thumb. But foreigners won't get off scot-free in the event of the dollar's demise, either. The world benefits from the use of one main currency—whether it is the dollar or another—because cross-border investment and trade costs fall when participants don't have to convert currencies repeatedly. An evolution to a euro bloc, a dollar bloc, and an Asian currency bloc, as some predict, may appeal to the world's sense of fairness. But it's likely to hurt everyone's wallet.

To my surprise, even Schinkel, the Dutch economics journalist, told me he never meant his film as a rallying cry for an end to the dollar standard. Rather, he insisted, it was meant to raise awareness about the complexity of the world financial system that has evolved under the dollar and, more important, to prod the United States to behave more fiscally responsible so that the currency wouldn't succumb to panic. "The system is good right now," he summed up. "It functions well. We would not be better off without the dollar."

* * *

As this book went to press in late 2007, the dollar was suffering what might be called an existential crisis.

For a currency that has served the world so well for so long, it was a bit alarming that no one had a kind word for it during its time of need. Middle Eastern countries that had linked their own currencies to the dollar for stability were changing policy. Investors who had turned to the dollar during times of market stress were questioning whether the buck was losing its traditional role as a "safe haven." America's critics, in particular, felt emboldened enough to lash out at the greenback, and indirectly at the United States itself. Venezuelan President Hugo Chávez urged his fellow OPEC members to dump the dollar and price oil in euros instead. "The fall of the dollar is not the fall of the dollar," Chávez declared in Riyadh, Saudi Arabia, at the end of the cartel's November meeting. "It's the fall of the American empire."

Washington wasn't doing much to defend the dollar's honor. Treasury Secretary Henry Paulson reiterated the government's long-held commitment to a "strong dollar," then seemed to undermine it by adding that market forces should determine the currency's value. What the market determined was that the dollar should fall. A lot. Spooked by an American credit crisis, a slowing economy and ballooning debt, traders sent the euro to several all-time highs against the dollar near the end of the year, while the Canadian "loonie" soared to levels against the dollar not seen since the 1800s.

Then the media piled on. In comic fashion, scores of journalists turned to popular culture figures to demonstrate just how unloved the dollar was. They pointed to a report that Brazilian supermodel Gisele Bündchen demanded to be paid in euros rather than dollars and referenced a video of hip-hop artist Jay-Z fanning stacks of 500-euro notes. Never mind that Gisele denied the story. Or that Jay-Z, not usually one associated with currency forecasting, was in all likelihood flashing the larger denominated bill merely for its own sake of excess. The times cried out for clear, accessible symbols of the dollar's demise, and these two did nicely.

Yet many failed to grasp that the dollar's rout in the foreign exchange market wasn't the same as toppling it as the world's most important currency. College football rankings may be determined every week, and the number one team is usually pushed aside if it suffers a stinging defeat. But currencies don't work that way. The dollar's anchoring role in international trade and as the main reserve currency for central banks is too ingrained to change overnight, even if the dollar's value erodes.

As one commentator in this book put it, currencies behave more like software operating systems. We as a society may decide that a better operating system exists than Microsoft Windows, the one most of us use. But there is a clear benefit of easy communication when we're all on the same system, whatever that system may be. Until our friends and business associates switch to a new and improved one, it won't do any of us much good to switch on our own.

That said, it's a good bet that one future day most computer users will shift to another operating system, and the dollar one day will likely give up its central role, too. If foreign creditors become wary of renewing their loans to the U.S. government, that day of reckoning could come a lot sooner than experts think.

But odds are the buck won't go down without a fight. The U.S. government would take extraordinary measures to prevent the sort of crisis that could dislodge the currency from its central role, one that has brought so many benefits to America. Other governments, fearing a collapse in the value of their own considerable dollar holdings, would have strong incentive to cooperate. Perhaps even Jay-Z would rise to the occasion with a new video, gleefully flashing a fat wad of Benjamins, old-school style.

At the time of this writing, the dollar's daily trading declined and the growing anxiety about its international position was shaping up as the currency's most trying period since the end of the gold standard in 1971. Yet there's no reason why the dollar won't get over its existential crisis. It just needs to come to grips with a reduced global role in the future. And sooner or later, most people will realize that even something less than the Almighty Dollar that the U.S. currency once was still looks better than any other immediate alternative.

—Craig Karmin, New York City, November 2007

CHAPTER 1

Fishing in the

Three-Trillion-Dollar Pond

I t was the kind of day that got people buzzing: a time, everyone knew, when big money could be won or lost. In trading rooms across the nation, normal activity had slowed to a crawl. Investors became hesitant to make any big moves before the news. Instead, coffee mugs were refilled. Sandwiches were munched on quietly at desks. Conversation twitched with nerves. Entire floors took on the atmosphere of a football locker room an hour before a big game, outwardly relaxed but taut, tense, and thick with anticipation. Trading rooms are usually hectic, crazy places with people screaming at each other or into phones. This morning's slow-boil intensity doesn't happen very often, and it was especially rare this time of year, when most desks were at half-staff, and those not yet on vacation were already thinking about the lazy days at beach houses or backyard barbecues to come. On this particular day, however, Tuesday, August 8, 2006, attention was tightly focused. The air was filled with the prospect of change.

"The Fed is front and center," Sue Herrera reminded her CNBC audience, at the top of the noon hour, with the breathless enthusiasm of a Super Bowl pregame host. "What will they do—or not do?"

Her audience needed no reminding. The Federal Reserve, led by its new and untested chairman, Ben Bernanke, would announce later that afternoon its decision on interest rates. For the past two years, primarily under the guidance of its legendary chairman Alan Greenspan, the Fed had methodically raised the so-called target for the Federal Funds rate (which determines commercial banks' overnight lending rates) to 5.25 percent from 1 percent. Those rate hikes were meant to cool off a fast-expanding economy and thereby snuff out any inflation.

But more recently, Bernanke had indicated he was developing a new concern: that of an economic slowdown—something that would be exacerbated by any further increase in rates. While inflation hawks insisted the Fed would continue with its rate hikes, the slowdown worry had some traders betting that the long cycle of increases was over and that Bernanke would leave rates alone. Such a seemingly innocuous move—the Fed simply announcing that it would do nothing—could mark a turn in the interest rate cycle, unleashing powerful reverberations across global financial markets. And for good reason. The level and direction of U.S. interest rates is a major factor in the pricing of stocks, bonds, and currencies around the world. What would the Fed do, or not do, indeed.

That afternoon in the midtown Manhattan office of FX Concepts, John R. Taylor Jr. was absorbed in his work. He appeared indifferent to the edginess around him in the trading room. He sat tall and regal in his swivel chair, his back to Sue Herrera and the TV. He had tuned out CNBC anyway. He wasn't taking calls, except from his wife, and he was largely ignoring the two dozen colleagues who circulated around him. Taylor was focused on a chart laid out on graph paper, moving a ruler over it from left to right, searching for a trend pattern between the euro and the dollar. "One more test of the downside and then you have a nice double bottom," he mumbled to himself.

Taylor is the founder, chairman, chief investment officer, and chief executive officer of this New York City–based hedge fund that specializes in foreign exchange trading. He manages money on behalf of large U.S. pension funds and endowments, as well as foreign governments, including Singapore and China. Overall, FX Concepts manages about $13 billion, making it one of the largest firms in the world to earn a living almost solely by betting on currencies. More precisely, the firm bets on the movements of the dollar and about thirty other currencies—from the majors like the euro and the yen to obscure ones like the Kenyan shilling and Peruvian nuevo sol—against one another.

Beyond Wall Street, London, Singapore, and a few other major financial centers, the foreign exchange market is followed far less regularly than the stock or bond market. Yet the currency market is the biggest market in the world, with a daily trading volume of $3.2 trillion (that compares with an average daily global stock market volume of about $300 billion). The amount of money exchanged in the currency market over a month's time is enough to buy all the goods and services the world produces over an entire year. Because FX Concepts is an active trader, and because it borrows money to increase the size of its bets, its influence is much greater than even its $13 billion in assets would indicate. The firm trades so much yen that a Japanese television crew filmed a mini-documentary

about Taylor and FX Concepts in 2005. Tokyo camera-
men hovered in a helicopter outside the firm's midtown
office to get long shots of the FX Concepts trading desk.
On some days, Taylor informed me, his firm's trading accounts for 1 percent of the total foreign exchange market's
activity. He is a very big fish in the biggest of all financial
ponds; and as a key player in the currency market, it is
people like him who help determine how much your dollars and my dollars are worth in the world.

Taylor and his firm had more riding on the Fed's decision than most, and his traders sat ready to act once the
Fed's decision came. But the CEO himself was looking
more at the big picture, and beyond the Fed's announcement. Taylor is a pioneer in the field of trend recogni-
tion: He uses computer models to examine the historical
relationships between currencies in order to predict how
those currencies are likely to trade in the months ahead.
At sixty-four years old, he works a sixty-hour week,
writes daily and weekly reports on the foreign exchange
market, travels abroad at least once a quarter, and oversees a staff of about sixty people in four countries.

Thanks to the currency business, he is also fabulously
wealthy, though growing up in the privileged environ-
ments of New York City and Long Island, he was never
a stranger to money. His credentials as a dyed-in-the-
wool New Yorker include the fact that he bought his
wife's engagement ring from a Manhattan jeweler who
turned out to be Woody Allen's father. There's a Waspish
sensibility to Taylor, who can trace his ancestors back to
the *Mayflower*. But there's also a surprisingly cantanker-
ous, anti-establishment edge to him that his soft patrician
features belie. His voice squeaks when he indulges in

conspiracy theories about the Bush administration (which is often) or derides a Wall Street analyst who dares spout conventional wisdom to him. He probably squeaked louder than ever when he was laid off by First National Bank of Chicago in 1974, an experience that would encourage him to start his own firm. Now he runs one of the more successful foreign exchange shops in the country. *Trader Monthly,* a glossy magazine that glorifies the pursuit of riches and the spoils of conspicuous consumption, ranked Taylor in 2004 as one of the one hundred wealthiest traders in the world. The magazine estimated Taylor's annual income at $30 million to $40 million, but he scoffs at that figure.

"I make an enormous amount of money, but not $30 million," Taylor told me in his office, the squeak in his voice rising slightly. Certainly, he makes enough to clothe himself in the Hermès ties, Alain Mikli eye glasses, stylish Italian cotton shirts, well-tailored blazers, and soft leather loafers he wears to the office each day (refusing to don the business-casual look of bright polo shirts and khaki pants popular with hedge fund traders). He makes enough to vacation in Italy each summer with his wife and son. He also makes enough to fund various side projects. These include a bomb-sniffing-dog business he started in Massachusetts after September 11 and Inspiration Biopharmaceuticals, a private company that is working to develop a cure for hemophilia. Phase-one trials for the company's drug are due to begin in the fall of 2007. Taylor's seventeen-year-old son suffers from this delayed-blood-clotting disease that leaves people vulnerable to hemorrhaging from even minor injuries.

So how much is an "enormous amount" of money? Taylor put it to me this way. During his undergraduate days at Princeton, Taylor's roommate was Charles Gibson, now anchor of ABC's *World News*. They still keep in touch, and Taylor says that a friendly rivalry has developed over the years about who can earn more money. "Charlie made $7 million last year," Taylor informed me, his gaze focused on a chart laid across his desk. "I beat him."

At 2:15 on the day of the Fed meeting, the long-awaited news arrived: The central bank announced that rates would indeed remain the same, ending the two-year period of unrelieved increases. But the Fed's publicly released statement seemed to leave open the possibility of future rate hikes. During the twelve hours that followed, as traders would think and rethink the Fed's next move, the dollar would go on a dramatic roller-coaster ride that offered a snapshot into how fickle the foreign exchange market can be: The dollar fell immediately after the Fed's announcement during New York trading, bounced back just before the end of the session, rallied powerfully during Asian trading hours, and finally gave back almost all those gains in the second half of the Far East session. When all was said and done, the dollar's value was roughly back to where it was before the Fed's decision. But in the rapid-fire world of foreign exchange, billions of dollars in trading profits could have been generated or could have disappeared.

For all the manic activity surrounding the Fed's decision, it is just one of many variables that can cause the currency market to gyrate wildly. Taylor and his team at FX Concepts allowed me to observe them over the second half of 2006. Along the way, Thailand suffered a military coup, the Dow Jones Industrial Average set several all-time highs, a plot to blow up planes flying from London to the United States was foiled, and North Korea claimed to have successfully tested a nuclear bomb. All these events, and many, many smaller ones, would express themselves in the currency market during those months. They caused the dollar's value to rise or fall, and not always in the way that Taylor or others in the market expected. Many times the dollar seemed to move forcefully for no reason whatsoever, as if the dollar's value was controlled by a grand, invisible puppeteer rather than the combined efforts of thousands of individual firms and players. But that's why figuring out how to make money in the $3.2-trillion-a-day foreign exchange market has caused so many firms to end in ruin. That's why it pays better than hosting a popular national evening news show.

* * *

FX Concepts's office is located across the street from Penn Station. Emerging from the subway stop, one is treated to a postcard view of the Empire State Building that's just two blocks away. Inside, the office is simple enough: wall clocks showing the time in Paris, Dubai, and Sydney (where FX Concepts used to have offices; Paris and Dubai are being replaced with London and Singapore, reflecting the firm's new outlets), a few long rows of desks, standard motel-issue beige carpet, and beige walls with blond trim. The cumulative effect of all that beige is somewhat soothing. Taylor said his previous office had a visitors' area where the curious could peek through glass windows at the trading floor to spy on the action. But he got rid of it because there was really nothing interesting to see. "There's no yelling here," he said. "No guys holding up two phones and screaming into them."

Jonathan Clark, Taylor's right-hand man, is especially soft-spoken. He starts each morning in Montclair, New Jersey, with three cups of espresso before boarding the commuter train that will take him to the FX Concepts office in Manhattan. Still boyish-looking at fifty-two, he is tan and has traces of blond in his sandy brown hair. Clark sits next to Taylor—and has for the past twenty-three years. He is more easygoing and, outwardly at least, more contemplative than his boss. But they work closely as a team of three: Taylor, Clark, and "the model."

Spend even one afternoon at FX Concepts and you will hear Clark and Taylor make repeated references to the model, as if there were a computer like HAL from Stanley Kubrick's *2001: A Space Odyssey* that they conversed with daily. Clark and Taylor would tell me things like, "the model says stand pat today" or "the model says buy more euros and sell dollars" or even "the model's not very happy with the market today." The model is a statistically driven computer program, proprietary and developed in-house, for analyzing currency movements over a variety of time periods. The firm trades billions of dollars every day according to what the model says.

In fact, it's not one model that tells them these things. FX Concepts relies on about twenty different models at a time, each looking at a different set of variables and relationships. In the minds of people at FX Concepts, currency movements are rarely random or unpredictable. They believe there is valuable knowledge to be gleaned

from the past, from the herd, from the seemingly contradictory signals financial markets give us. While currency
players, events, and trading volume may change, historical trading patterns are pretty constant. If you can identify these patterns in their early stages, they believe, you
can forecast a currency's future direction. According to
Clark, "The model picks up subtle changes in a currency
just before a big move or reversal—changes that are too
obscure for the rest of us to notice."

The decisions of all the models are aggregated so FX
Concepts can decide whether it should buy or sell the
dollar versus another currency. For instance, when de-
ciding to buy dollars and sell yen (or to do the reverse),
one model will analyze the relationship between American and Japanese interest rates, another will examine the
price history of the two currencies' trading, and a third
will slice and dice the amount of volatility in yen-dollar
trading. Taken together, FX Concepts decided to buy
dollars and to sell yen for much of 2006.

It is a sign of how much more active and complex the
foreign exchange market is today than two decades ago
that FX Concepts started with just three of these models
to predict currency movements in 1981. Taylor dumped
the oldest of those original three models at the end of
2006. Even the existing models that have served him
well remain works in progress. He says that the models
have particular trouble predicting currency movements
accurately during periods when a central bank raises interest rates rapidly, and he's still not sure why that is.
During the firm's worst year, 1994, a time when the
Federal Reserve raised rates eight times in quick succes-
sion, FX Concepts's flagship fund had a return that year

of negative 19 percent. The fund rebounded with one of its best returns, up 35 percent, the following year. But the glitch in the model remains a concern.

Taylor and Clark also believe in the power of charts, which they use to consider revisions to the models or to supplement the models' findings. Clark's cubicle is cluttered with graph paper, computer printouts, and, most of all, piles and piles of charts. The charts usually show how certain currencies have traded against each other. To the uninformed they look like the sort of geometry proofs that stumped all but the A-plus students. But where others might see inscrutable pinwheel shapes or clusters of dots, Clark and Taylor see patterns—historical relationships that leap from the page as if outlined in fluorescent light. They see truth. In the technical lingo of FX Concepts, Clark and Taylor aim to spot "double or triple bottoms" or "wedges" or perhaps a "head-and-shoulders." They also use mathematical equations, like Fibonacci relationships, to forecast currency moves. "Those can be notoriously difficult to recognize," Clark said. "There's often a false break before reversing."

While FX Concepts relies on computer-driven models to analyze piles of data, it's Clark and Taylor's job to oversee the model and tweak its recommendations—to make sure the firm isn't taking too large risks on any trade. The computer, for instance, has been so bearish on yen that it instructs a sale of the Japanese currency that's bigger, and therefore riskier, than the firm feels comfortable doing. "We are short yen up to our eyeballs," Clark told me, meaning the firm has bet that the yen will depreciate against the dollar, the euro, and other currencies. "That makes us nervous." Even though he decided to bet a little less against the yen than the model instructed, FX Concepts was short about $2 billion in yen in early August of 2006.

At the opposite end of the spectrum, the model's favorite currency was Iceland's krona. Iceland had run up a massive trade deficit that was frightening off foreign investors, and this rapid exodus had punished the currency during the first half of 2006. But more recently, the krona was strengthening on signs that it was oversold and because of the high interest rates Iceland offered. So FX Concepts was among the world's biggest buyers of krona: The model called for 15 percent of the firm's total capital to be bet on a tiny Scandinavian nation of 300,000 people. "We have $650 for every man, woman, and child in Iceland," Taylor told me. He scaled down that bet to about 13 percent of the firm's capital to avoid such a large concentration in a country with a population the size of Toledo, Ohio.

This approach to foreign exchange trading, known as trend following, is commonly used on Wall Street, at least to some degree. But few rely on trend watching to the same extent that FX Concepts does, and few spend the time and put forth the effort to build their own models. There are many other factors that traders dissect when picking currencies. They track large cross-border capital flows by central banks and the actions of other substantial institutional investors. Some look at international data and favor the currencies of countries with large trade surpluses and sell the currencies of countries with large trade deficits. The country with the deficit, the reasoning goes, will want to allow its currency to weaken so that its goods become more globally competitive and its trade deficit is reduced. Other trading shops focus more broadly on equating a strong economy with a strong currency and spend their time parsing economic data to determine which currencies to bet on. Clark, however, is skeptical that models can be built around this sort of strategy. "If you try to model economic growth differentials, it doesn't work," Clark said dismissively. And without an effective model, he reasoned, it's mostly guesswork. Or simply gambling.

FX Concepts, however, is not purely about number crunching. A few people at the firm are experts in their fields and accomplished authors. They have published works about foreign exchange trading, derivatives, and pension fund reform. Even Taylor, in his weekly client dispatches, usually takes a step back from the market and muses on current events or history, putting his doctorate work in political economy at the University of North Carolina to work. One August report titled "The Rich Get Richer and the Poor Get Poorer" was a not-entirely-unique condemnation of the economy in President Bush's America, though the criticism was a bit unusual coming from a hedge fund elite. But don't think he's too left-wing. Another report, "La Dolce Vita," penned while Taylor was vacationing in Rome, drew parallels between China's Communist Party and Mussolini's fascist regime.

• • •

Currency trading is different from any other type of financial market. When an investor buys a stock or bond, he or she owns an underlying asset and a future income stream. In the case of a stock, the investor owns shares in a company and, in many instances, receives regular dividend payments. In the case of a bond, he or she is a creditor to a company or a government and receives regular interest payments for that loan. Foreign exchange traders don't typically own an asset. Rather, they make a bet that the price of one currency will strengthen or weaken in relation to another. That also means that there is no such thing as a bull or bear market for foreign exchange: Currencies only strengthen or weaken relative to one another. So some are always rising and some are always falling.

Foreign exchange has another important difference. With the explosion of global trade over the past two decades and with the world's stock markets moving more in sync with one another than perhaps ever before, currency movements tend to be less extreme than they used to be. While individual stocks can see their values double or triple or fall in half during a given year, the major currencies like the dollar, euro, yen, British pound, and Swiss franc typically strengthen or weaken only about 5 percent to 15 percent against each other over a twelve-month period.

Currency traders therefore aim to amplify those relatively modest movements with borrowed money, known as leverage. Under this system, banks or brokers provide currency funds like FX Concepts with loans that allow them to bet an amount that is several multiples greater than the firm's actual assets. Analysts say for hedge funds this can range from ratios of four to twelve times (or in some cases, even more) the amount of money they actually have under management. Leverage at these ratios can turn a modest 5 percent currency gain into a profit of 20 percent to 60 percent. But it's not a risk-free proposition. The once high-flying hedge fund Amaranth Advisors LLC suffered billions of dollars in losses in 2006 that were directly related to bad bets that became catastrophic because of borrowed money. The firm reportedly had leverage of about five-to-one for its unsuccessful wagers on the direction of natural gas prices.

Despite the risks, more investors are involved with betting on currency movements than ever before. Daily trading volume, which was around $500 billion in 1989, has risen sixfold to $3.2 trillion. Widespread predictions that foreign exchange volume would dry up with the introduction of the euro—when a dozen individual currencies were replaced with a common one—proved misguided. The introduction of the widely used euro seemed only to generate greater interest in the market.

Several factors lie behind this surge in foreign exchange trading. The increased use of leverage means that the same number of trades can involve many more dollars. Advances in computer technology enable traders to get better prices and attract new participants into the market, including retail investors. Perhaps most of all, the continuing expansion of international trade has been a boon to the currency market. Increased international trade means more and more companies have to convert their overseas sales from foreign to local currencies.

Then there's the trend that FX Concepts is following most closely: Many of America's largest and most conservative institutional investors are changing their ways. Historically, big investors like pension funds and endowments have kept the bulk of their money in American stocks and bonds, where they are among the market's biggest investors. But the bursting of the tech bubble in 2000 made many pension funds wary of putting too much money in stocks. Meanwhile, bonds have been paying out less in regular interest payments, thanks to the gradual decline in Treasury yields. This situation has put the average pension fund in a bind. With benefit costs rising, many have been forced to pay out more money than they are taking in. So these funds are sniffing around for a new way to amplify their returns. Some have turned to foreign stocks and emerging markets. Others have turned to private equity and real estate. And some have turned to hedge funds and the foreign exchange market as the answer.

"Getting a meeting with pension funds in the past was very hard when clients were getting 20 percent returns from stocks," Dr. Arun Muralidhar, a managing director at FX Concepts who works directly with pension funds, told me. "Now, these pension funds are actively looking for managers who know currencies." Recently, for example, FX Concepts added $2 billion in assets from the Pennsylvania Public School Employees Retirement System.

The pension funds' nascent interest in currency trading comes at a curious period for FX Concepts. Taylor's firm has a proud track record for performance since it began managing money in the late 1980s: The flagship fund, Developed Market Currency (DMC) Program, boasts an average annual return of 11 percent since its inception in 1989, and perhaps more important, it suffered only one year of negative returns during its first fourteen years. Over the past three years, however, it has been struggling through its toughest stretch in two and a half decades. An ill-advised bet on the dollar's rise in 2004 contributed to a 2 percent decline in 2004, and the fund eked out only a modest 3 percent return in 2005. By the middle of 2006, the DMC fund was again floundering in negative territory.

Taylor looked a bit unnerved at the thought of another down year—now was the time to impress the growing list of potential clients with stellar returns that would attract them to the fund. The $2 billion from the Pennsylvania teachers was great, but another bad year of performance might discourage other pension funds. And he was at something of a loss to explain the fund's recent slump. Still, he said, a cardinal sin in trading is to lose your nerve and to change your position too early. The big bets against the yen and purchases of the Icelandic krona would stay, as would a new position betting on a rebound in the dollar. "The name of the game is to walk as close to the cliff as possible," he said in a low voice. "Stopping before the edge of the cliff costs you money."

·   ·   ·

The evening of August 8, a few hours after the Fed's decision to leave interest rates unchanged, Jeff Weiser settled in for a good meal. The currency trader from FX Concepts was joined by three of his colleagues and by a group of sales brokers from one of the major Wall Street firms. They were seated at Rosa Mexicano, a trendy midtown restaurant. The most upscale place for Mexican cuisine in Manhattan, the restaurant is famous for its pomegranate margaritas and the extra-chunky guacamole that waiters mash tableside. This was a casual meeting, meant as a way for everyone to get to know one another better. Neckties were loosened, and a few rounds of drinks were ordered as the discussion turned toward what the Fed's next move might be. FX Concepts traders were enjoying their margaritas, and Weiser was "powering down some guacamole," as he put it to me the next morning, when around 7:00 P.M., everyone's cell phones started sounding at once, like a series of alarm bells going off. And, in effect, that's exactly what they were.

Trading had opened in Asia and the dollar was staging an unexpectedly powerful rally against most of the Pacific Rim currencies. The FX Concepts traders were all being paged by their contacts on Wall Street, who wanted to know if they were interested in trading during this big dollar rally. Weiser excused himself from the table and scanned the noisy restaurant for somewhere he could have a bit of privacy and quiet. He needed to shake off the effects of his drink and think fast about what to do. Even more important, he wanted to be out of earshot of the sales brokers at his table. FX Concepts took huge positions in some of the currencies that Weiser traded, and although this was a friendly meeting, he knew that Wall Street people would be keen to know his moves. Such information would be valuable both to themselves and to their other clients.

Hunched over his cell phone by the men's restroom, Weiser instructed his broker to buy $20 million worth of dollars (known as "20 bucks" in traders' lingo) and to sell yen. He also sold some euros against the dollar. Then he went back to the table to see if the food had arrived. "The tone of the dinner had changed," Weiser recalled.

The jovial mood was broken. "Some of us at the table were making money. And some of us were not."

Welcome to the nonstop world of a foreign exchange trader. While big American companies may have shares that also trade in Tokyo and London, traders know that to get the best price on Microsoft or General Motors, they have to wait for the New York session. Likewise, traders prefer to grab or unload U.S. Treasury bonds during American trading hours. Greenwich mean time is when they like to buy or sell metals. Foreign exchange is the only financial market in which trading is steady all day long, and traders are largely indifferent to time zones.

This enviable status reflects, in part, the dollar's privileged position in the world. The U.S. currency is part of nearly 90 percent of all foreign exchange transactions. If, for instance, someone wants to trade Mexican pesos for Czech crowns, both currencies will likely be converted to dollars first and then converted back to complete the trade. And because plenty of dollars are found everywhere in the world, the currency market can operate equally effectively during Singapore or London trading as New York. It is a big reason why foreign exchange is the one truly twenty-four-hour trading bazaar—one that all other financial markets hope somehow to one day replicate.

From the moment New Zealand begins trading at 2:00 P.M. eastern standard time on Sunday until New York trading finishes around 4:00 P.M. on Friday, currency traders are on duty. Global investment banks like Morgan Stanley or Merrill Lynch have large staffs in every corner of the world, and when trading in the Pacific time zone ends, the "book"—a list of the banks' positions in every currency—is passed on to their colleagues in London, who then pass the book on to their counterparts in New York.

But for a hedge fund like FX Concepts, the traders are on call day and night. Sleep and socializing are something they do between buy and sell orders. An earthquake in Japan at midnight EST? Expect a phone call, and you should know your yen positions and what you want to do, pronto, before the market moves against you. A surprise rate increase from the Bank of England at 4:00 A.M. EST? Wake up sleepyhead—what do you want to do about your pound sterling position? It's the sort of job where one day bleeds into the next because the trading day doesn't ever end. It just rolls along, following the sun from one region of the world to another.

Taylor and the model may decide which currencies to own and which to dump, but it's up to guys like Weiser to carry out those instructions by making the necessary trades in the open market. Weiser also has some discretion on trades, giving him the flexibility to deviate slightly (and usually temporarily) from what the model says if he spots a particularly attractive opportunity. That's why he's often up at twilight hours, hoping to find a deal. He's the embodiment of the City That Never Sleeps.

At thirty-seven years old, with pale blue eyes and dark, thinning hair, Weiser embraces the mania of his job. The first thing you notice when meeting him is that he stands less than four feet tall. The second thing is that, despite this diminutive stature, he's a commanding presence in the room. Weiser is among the first to arrive each morning at 7:00 A.M., and he can be spotted frequently scurrying across the floor to relay information to Taylor and Clark. When he hoists himself up on top of a desk to adjust the office air-conditioning dial, he's greeted with a smattering of quiet applause. But usually, Wesier can be found at his cubicle, chatting with brokers, checking prices and news on his screens, or punching in data with fingers a little too stubby for comfortable use of the keys. He began his trading career at FX Concepts in 1999, and today he is responsible for thirty-two currencies. He is one of seven traders on twenty-four-hour duty. He is often awakened after midnight, he says, or he is up checking news and his currency positions half the night. A few times a month he'll be summoned even later, maybe 3:00 A.M. or 4:00 A.M. He's conditioned himself to awaken at full alertness, at any hour, the moment his phone rings.

Weiser is typically in the office for about ten straight hours, and since he and the other traders can never be away from a phone or a price screen for long, FX Concepts installed a full gym in a corner of the office, which Weiser uses a three days a week. His personal trainer urges him on as he lifts Cybex weights or jogs on the treadmill. All the while, he's watching currency movements on a Reuters screen that flashes on the gym's plasma TV. His Manhattan apartment is equipped with a Reuters terminal that delivers currency prices in real time so that he can trade as easily at home as in the office.

As a bachelor, or self-professed "single dude," Weiser has an easier time complying with the demands of this erratic schedule than colleagues who are married with kids. "But we all adapt to that sort of behavior," he said. Weiser won't turn off the lights at night until he has a plan for what to do with his positions under a variety of scenarios—in case there's a big overnight event that would affect the markets. "I haven't had a night where I slept like a rock in six years."

Indeed, the evening of the Fed meeting, it turned out the action at Rosa Mexicano was only the beginning. At 9:00 P.M., he got a call at his home from Taylor. The boss instructed him to sell more euros. Then something weird happened. At about 3:00 A.M., when the markets in London were poised to open, the dollar suddenly, and for no apparent reason, turned south and began erasing all the gains it had chalked up during the Pacific session. Weiser's phone started ringing from brokers in Tokyo, Singapore, and London. He decided not to make any trades on the news, and he went back to sleep. But it was a restless sleep, and he awoke again around 4:30 A.M. to check news and prices on his computer terminal. Astonishingly, the dollar was back to the same levels it had been when he left the office the previous afternoon. "I realized then that I could have turned my phone off when I left the office, ignored all this noise, and my positions would have been exactly the same," he said, somewhat ruefully. So he slipped back beneath the covers until the alarm clock rang at 6:00 A.M.

While being a trader is considered a hardcore financial job, it can also require putting on a political analyst hat. Two days after the Fed meeting, a broker in Tokyo rang up Weiser at 1:30 in the morning. British officials had just announced the arrest of twenty-four people they alleged were planning a terrorist plot to blow up jetliners flying from London to the United States. The British pound was nose-diving on fears that some of the suspected terrorists were still at large and could be plotting another attack. The Swiss franc, frequently considered a safe haven in times of uncertainty, was rallying. What, the Tokyo broker inquired, did Weiser want to do?

Nothing much, he decided. He called another brokerage contact to see if anyone thought something bigger was going on—if there were any rumors that the British authorities hadn't revealed everything. "Personally, I thought the news was good—something was *not* blowing up," he said that morning in the office. He thought the markets were particularly volatile at the moment and that the losses in the pound could reverse powerfully at any moment, just as the dollar changed course unexpectedly a couple of days ago. He held pat. After about thirty minutes, he was back asleep.

A couple of months later, Weiser was forced to analyze an even more menacing potential crisis. All day on Friday, October 6, the market was rife with rumors and speculative reports that North Korea was on the verge of a nuclear bomb test. If the rumors proved true, they would raise anxiety about safety in South Korea, Japan, and much of the Pacific Rim. So Weiser wanted to reduce some of his South Korean won and other Asian currency positions before the weekend. But every other trader was looking to do the same, and the cheap prices being offered for Asian currencies reflected that. Weiser had a tough choice: dump part of his Asian position at a terrible price but at least be covered in the event of a nuclear explosion or take a chance that the rumors were wrong and wait until prices improved next week. "I decided to stick with what I had and hope nothing happened," Weiser recalled.

For most of the weekend, it looked like the right call. Nothing but silence from Pyongyang. Then, around

8:00 P.M. EST on Sunday, the phone calls started coming: first from Deutsche Bank and then Goldman Sachs. Finally, news stories confirming North Korea's claim of a successful bomb test hit the newswires around 10:30 P.M. "I was still patting myself on the back when the bomb went off," Weiser said regretfully. "I bought some dollars and sold some won on the news—but only a small amount because I wasn't sure the news was correct."

He stayed up until 1:00 A.M., buying some Taiwanese dollars that he thought looked cheap. Then he ordered his brokers to wake him if the dollar rose or fell by 1 percent or more against the won. But his geopolitical read was that North Korea's nuclear test was not the watershed event that others made it out to be. "North Korea isn't going to explode a bomb and then turn around and attack South Korea," he told me a few days later in his office, his feet dangling from his seat a few inches above the floor. "They want negotiating power. I don't think it changes the political climate in the world." He was confident enough about this decision that he went quickly back to sleep after his 1:00 A.M. purchases.

"Funnily enough, after a nuclear explosion, I slept like a baby that night," he said, chuckling. "When was the last time that happened?"

.   .   .

Foreign exchange may be the biggest financial market in the world, but it's also one of the newest. Throughout the nineteenth and the first half of the twentieth century, the world's major currencies were tied to a gold standard, rather than trading directly against one another in an open market. In 1944, the Bretton Woods agreement established the dollar at the center of the world financial system by fixing it at a rate of $35 per ounce of gold. All the other major currencies were then set at a fixed rate to the dollar. There was no need for a foreign exchange market because all major currencies were pegged to a dollar rate and could only be changed in unusual circumstances and only with the permission of the International Monetary Fund. This changed in 1971, when President Nixon took the dollar off the gold standard. By negating the Bretton Woods agreement, the president had freed up other currencies to trade more freely against the dollar and one another.

By 1973, an incipient foreign exchange market had developed, where the value of one currency was determined relative to the value of others. The number of active participants, however, was still small and consisted mostly of international banks and large exporters, such as automakers like Ford Motor Company or giant conglomerates like General Electric, that were interested in hedging their foreign currency risk. It was around this time that John Taylor decided that there was a future in learning how to forecast currency movements.

Taylor's interest in finance and investment was sparked at an early age. As a thirteen-year-child in Long Island, his father gave him $7,000. This was no play money. "He told me, 'Invest wisely. This is your college fund.'" Not knowing the first thing about investing but eager to learn, the boy researched companies through the newspaper and from brokerage research his father brought him. Taylor favored stocks that paid regular dividends. One of his first selections was the MKT

Railroad, a railway company in bankruptcy at the time but one that owned land that some analysts said was worth more than the $4.00 stock price. When he sold the stock a few months later, the share price had more than doubled to $9.00.

With proceeds from his stock market investments, Taylor paid for part of his college tuition at Princeton University, where he studied European civilization. Still, away from academia, his interest in investing and markets continued. His first job out of college was working as a financial analyst at Citibank. "But I didn't like taking orders or selling stock," he squeaked. "That wasn't very interesting." He moved to Chemical Bank to work in a lending office, though he was still not very satisfied. Here, at least, Taylor convinced his boss to pay for business school classes uptown at Columbia University.

Columbia would provide his first real break. He studied the embryonic world of foreign exchange trading, learning that currency values were essentially reflections of how markets viewed the strength of one economy versus another. Impressed with Taylor's enthusiasm for the new foreign exchange market, one of his Columbia professors recommended the Chemical Bank junior loan officer contribute a chapter to a new compendium the bank was preparing on currency trading. Taylor wrote about early foreign exchange trading strategies for the book, which was distributed in 1972 to Chemical's corporate clients and to American business schools. It was one of the first texts on the subject, and though foreign exchange was limited by trading bands that prevented currencies from moving too far in one direction or another, the book anticipated a future when the major currencies would trade almost as freely as stocks and bonds. The publication also helped Taylor's star rise at the bank. He was put in charge of Chemical's foreign exchange consulting business, where he analyzed currency risk and offered forecasts. It wasn't long before Taylor quickly established himself as an authority in the fledgling, wild frontier of currency trading.

The next year, he moved to Chicago to accept a new position at First National Bank of Chicago. His clients were primarily multinational corporations. They were trying to understand the ramifications of a bold new world where currencies traded against one another—a world where a weakening currency in an overseas market could slash that foreign subsidiary's profits. Not only did Taylor help clients understand how to hedge their positions with derivatives to protect themselves from currency weakness, he also began working with more aggressive clients who sought to make additional profits in their overseas subsidiaries with some side bets on currency movements. Further, he speculated on currencies on behalf of First National Bank. One day in 1974, he helped the bank make $15 million with a successful wager that Australia would devalue its dollar. It was one of the most profitable bets that had been made on a currency move at the time.

But Taylor's aggressive style in this rapidly developing market didn't sit well with everyone at First National Bank. He was laid off after just fifteen months in Chicago. (Though in true trader fashion, he managed to make money even in being fired. He bet colleagues weeks before his dismissal that he was about to be let go.) Despite this apparent setback, Taylor hurt neither for money nor opportunity. He had three job offers within twenty-four hours and decided to return to Citibank in New York to head up their new, and still struggling, foreign exchange department. One of the first things Taylor did was to hire away eighteen people from First National Bank who had worked for him in Chicago. His team of thirty then set out to develop new trading methods and strategies.

In December 1976, Taylor and his team executed what is thought to be the first currency swap, a type of financial derivative in which two parties exchange currencies with each other at an agreed upon interest rate and time period. They were often carried out as a way to get around a particular country's foreign exchange controls. In this case, Citibank created a five-year swap for Corning Glass and a British counterpart for £20 million. The American company made a $880,000 profit on the swap. Under Taylor's guidance, Citi was rapidly developing into a major force in the foreign exchange market. When he rejoined the bank in 1974, it ranked just eighth among U.S. banks in currency trading volume. Four years later, Citi had catapulted to number one.

Taylor felt restless nonetheless. He ran a big team, but as part of a giant financial organization, he still did not feel independent enough. The memory of his abrupt, unceremonious exit from First National Bank—despite the profits he had generated for a firm he considered ungrateful—was never far from his mind. Would he ever have real job security or independence at a major bank, one full of ambitious and politically shrewd superiors? Besides, as Taylor put it bluntly, "I got paid so little I couldn't afford to live in New York." So Taylor cleared out his desk at Citibank for a second time and left to start his own firm.

That firm was called Emcore, and Taylor launched it in 1979 with $12,000 and two partners who had worked with him at Citi and had also grown disenchanted at the bank. Emcore provided foreign exchange research and economic forecasting to corporate clients. But Taylor's cantankerous nature got the best of him even here, at a tiny firm at which no one could fire him and he was but one of a small staff. So, in 1981, he sold his share of the company and then launched FX Concepts. While he took on a partner, Taylor controlled 80 percent of this new business and was finally his own boss. Now he could call all the shots. This firm started out with a business plan similar to that of Emcore, and he advised big exporters, including Coca-Cola, Eastman Kodak, R. J. Reynolds, and Armstrong Cork on how to protect their sales from currency fluctuations. Six years later, FX Concepts boasted revenue of $7 million.

Still, he wasn't quite satisfied. Taylor was growing more and more intrigued by the foreign exchange market, but he was growing increasingly bored with the consulting business. The real money, he knew, was made from being a player—from placing your own bets on currencies and following through on your forecasts, not from collecting the table scraps left over after some huge conglomerate had made a bundle shorting the New Zealand dollar or swapping yen for Deutsche marks. "We wanted to manage money," Taylor recalled. "We wanted to have big institutional clients. The problem was, there weren't really many institutional clients who wanted to bet on the foreign exchange market."

In 1987, Taylor finally convinced one client—Kodak—to let FX Concepts manage money on the company's behalf, buying and selling currencies for the camera maker and helping it hedge positions for its foreign stock portfolio. Not long after, the New York–based brokerage firm Lehman Brothers hired Taylor to actively buy and sell currencies on its behalf. Within a couple of years, FX Concepts had $1 billion under management, virtually all of it used to bet on the rise or fall of the dollar and the other major currencies. Taylor was no longer just a consultant but a currency speculator. At last, he would have the money to live in New York. And then some.

.   .   .

As an active participant in the foreign exchange market, FX Concepts had become a hedge fund. For many people unfamiliar with how most hedge funds operate, the term is often a loaded one—associated with secret dealings and attacks on currencies or companies. This impression has been re-enforced by the fact that hedge funds are not required to register with the Securities and Exchange Commission (this is because they are available only to institutions or other so-called sophisticated investors, such as wealthy individuals). While the reality is that most operate as ethically as a mutual fund or any other investment manager, hedge funds are allowed to take more risks than mutual funds, and they often do so. And perhaps no hedge funds have done more to promote the image of these money managers as swashbuckling, take-no-prisoner financial pirates than the ones that place massive bets on currencies.

Though well known today, hedge funds were still in relative infancy in the 1980s, and the public perception of hedge funds that bet on currencies was shaped largely by a few high-profile men, like Julian Robertson and his Tiger Fund and George Soros, known as the "Man Who Broke the Bank of England." In 1992, his funds sold short more than $10 billion worth of British pounds. Soros was betting that the Bank of England would be reluctant to protect its currency by raising interest rates. That would only further aggravate the country's recession, he figured. Instead, he bet, England would be forced to withdraw the pound from the European Exchange Rate Mechanism, a monetary system that was the precursor to the euro. Unable to keep up with Soros, and other speculators who joined him in betting against the pound, the Bank of England eventually capitulated, removing the pound from the European monetary system so that it could devalue the currency. That day became known in England as "Black Wednesday."

The central bank's retreat was a humiliation for the United Kingdom. British government officials had repeatedly assured the public that they would stand up to speculators. Toward that end, the Bank of England had bought billions of pounds, using precious foreign reserves in an effort to crush Soros and other hedge fund managers. The day after the Bank of England surrendered, a columnist at the London *Times* wrote that "millions of Britons woke up this morning to read with horror about the devaluation of sterling, the utter collapse of the government's economic policy, the personal humiliation of the Prime Minister and Chancellor, and generally Britain's relegation to the third league of banana republics." Soros, meanwhile, was said to have pocketed more than $1 billion from that trade.

While Soros may have been admired in the investment world for his financial savvy and the guts it took to put up so much money, many governments were less enthralled with the Man Who Broke the Bank of England and with currency speculators in general. They didn't like the idea that private money managers could have such powerful influence over their monetary policy and their currency's global value.

Indeed, during the Asian financial crisis in 1997, Soros's foreign exchange trading would be in the headlines again. It featured as part of the most public feud ever between a currency speculator and head of state. The trouble started when Malaysia's ringgit tumbled 20 percent against the dollar over a two-month period, causing heavy losses in the country's stock and bond markets. Former Malaysian prime minister Dr. Mohamed Mahathir told the press his currency's collapse was the fault of global capitalism. As the crisis deepened, Mahathir became increasingly specific. He blamed first currency speculators, then Jewish speculators, and finally Soros in particular (who happens to be Jewish and who survived the Nazi occupation of his native Hungary).

Mahathir even assigned a motive to Soros. The former prime minister said the speculator aimed to punish Malaysia for political reasons. Soros had recently lobbied the Association of Southeast Asian Nations (ASEAN) to reject Myanmar's bid to join the economic club, citing the country's controversial record on human rights.

Malaysia ignored this plea and played a prominent role in welcoming Myanmar into ASEAN. Myanmar's membership in the club was behind Soros's vengeful currency sales, Mahathir alleged.

At the September 1997 World Bank meeting in Hong Kong, Mahathir publicly vented these accusations. He never mentioned Soros by name this time, but everyone knew whom he meant when he referred to those "whose wealth must come from impoverishing others . . . I am saying that currency trading is unnecessary, unproductive, and totally immoral. It should be stopped." Soros, who all along had insisted that his fund was in fact *buying* ringgit on the theory that the currency had become oversold, fired back against the former Malaysian prime minister: "Dr. Mahathir's suggestion yesterday to ban currency trading is so inappropriate that it does not deserve serious consideration. Interfering with the convertibility of capital at a moment like this is a recipe for disaster. Dr. Mahathir is a menace to his own country."

As a speculator who profited mightily from bets on Asian currency declines during the 1997 financial crisis, Taylor was one of the hedge fund managers that Mahathir publicly blasted, if only indirectly. Although he's one of the biggest traders worldwide in several currencies, from the Chilean peso to the Icelandic krona, Taylor said he's never been singled out for the wrath of government officials. But there is no doubt that many government officials, abroad as well as some in Washington, would agree with at least some of what Mahathir charged—that private investment funds wield too much power and are not accountable enough to the public. With many hedge funds believing that the dollar is in a secular decline, Taylor has little doubt that his fund and others would take a good part of the blame if the dollar were to collapse. "If the dollar goes into a freefall, interest rates will probably rise, oil prices will go up, and the U.S. would go into recession," he said. "Politicians could easily blame hedge funds for the mess."

· · ·

The month of September, Taylor told me just before the start of the Labor Day weekend 2006, is traditionally an "explosive time" in the foreign exchange market. Summer is effectively over. Traders are all back from vacation. Perhaps most important, it's the month when clients often have new money they are looking to invest. FX Concepts and its main competitors were all looking forward to fresh funds coming in. A concern was that some of this new money would have to go into small markets and that prices could get distorted by big waves of cash. "I've got to start investing tomorrow," he squeaked. It was going to require finesse.

September turned out to be a pretty bad month. The declines among FX Concepts's various funds ranged from 2.7 percent to 9.7 percent over the four-week period—substantial losses for one month in the currency market. The yen did not fall as much as Taylor and his model expected it would. That afternoon, however, Taylor said he was undeterred. He's continuing with a big yen short position. FX Concepts, like many of its peers, also has a fund that bets not on a particular currency's direction, but that the market as a whole will experience large swings in prices. This is known as betting on market volatility. It is done through buying certain derivatives. Yet, despite a Thai government coup, the liquidation of Amaranth Advisors hedge fund, North Korea's nuclear test, and OPEC production cuts, the foreign exchange market has remained maddeningly calm. That has caused Taylor's bets on rising volatility to go sour. With all the changes in the foreign exchange market over the past several years, some analysts think that trend following and modeling may be struggling to keep up—that the market is evolving faster than the models that predict currency movements can. Even Taylor admits that some of the firm's earliest models are no longer effective.

But Taylor is not ready to concede another down year—not yet, anyway. And he's looking to the dollar to salvage his 2006. He's betting that the dollar has one last rally in it. "The model says right now we should be very long the dollar," he told me in early October. On the surface, it looked like a strange move. Certainly, Taylor's pessimism about the dollar's fate in the year ahead is well known. In his 2006 weekly market comments, he predicted numerous times that the U.S. housing market faces a slowdown and that there would likely be an accompanying recession in 2007, perhaps a severe one. Such a scenario would be bleak for the dollar. But Taylor's willingness to bet on the greenback in early October illustrates how currency speculators often care more about predicting the short-term behavior of the crowd than they do about the longer-term prospects for currencies—especially if the funds are trend followers like FX Concepts.

So far, 2006 had been a mildly disappointing year for the U.S. currency. Over the first nine months, the U.S.

Dollar Index, which measures the dollar's performance against a trade-weighted basket of six major currencies, had fallen 6 percent. The marginal declines reflected modest but growing concerns about the U.S. economy. Traders believed the U.S. economy was slowing and that the Fed would eventually be compelled to lower interest rates. If U.S. rates fell, the gap with lower European and Japanese rates would narrow, and U.S. assets would lose their yield advantage. That was expected to have a direct and negative impact on the dollar.

Before that happens, Taylor is counting on "the dollar's last hurrah" to lift his funds back into positive territory. At the start of the month, this strategy seemed to be working. When I visited Taylor in his office on October 10, the dollar was at its best level of the year against the yen and at a two-and-a-half-month high versus the euro. The U.S. currency was rallying on surprisingly strong economic data, such as a rare gain in national wages, that some saw as evidence that fears of a slowdown were overstated. "Wage gains are a false sign of prosperity," Clark said confidently. "They often come at the end of an economic boom."

Still, they might give the Fed a reprieve from feeling compelled to cut interest rates. This was, in Taylor's mind, a market misperception he would try to exploit—a bogus optimism that would carry the dollar a bit higher before the economic data made the case for a U.S. recession too plain for the market or the Fed to ignore. His plan was, in effect, to jump on the pro-dollar bandwagon and hope he could jump off again before everyone else tried to do the same. FX Concepts had increased its dollar bets over the past seventy-two hours, prior to our meeting, in particular against the euro, yen, and Swiss franc. "It's all a big head fake, this dollar rally," Taylor said to me with a shrug. "But we're out on a limb now with the dollar."

•   •   •

By November 1, the dollar's gains looked to be petering out. With each new set of economic data painting an ever-gloomier picture, the U.S. currency had tumbled over the past several days versus the yen, euro, and other major currencies. Taylor had always been planning to shift against the dollar before year-end. But the greenback's abrupt reversal this soon seemed to have caught him off guard. FX Concepts's flagship fund had been rising high in October, up 4 percent by mid-month. Then the dollar turned, and the fund was lucky to escape with a 1 percent gain on the month. In an effort to walk close to the edge of the cliff, Taylor looked perilously close to falling off it. "We were looking for a turn in the dollar on November 13," he said of the model, shaking his head dejectedly with the air of a disappointed father. "But it looks like the boat has already turned."

So FX Concepts turned with it. Titanic cruise ships may not be able to change course quickly, but nimble $13 billion hedge funds can. They simply close down positions, call in their bets, and reverse direction. Taylor and his model were now convinced that the big dollar sell-off had arrived and they would count on that move as a way to save them from another sub-par year. He even cut back on his massive short bet against the yen, expecting it now to pick up ground versus the dollar.

"We are now big-dollar bears," Taylor said. "I feel this is the real thing." But did he really? For the first time since I'd met him, I sensed a bit of desperation creeping into his squeaky voice. He was betraying an uncharacteristic lack of conviction in his model and in his own gut—in instincts that had been honed over decades of forecasting and trading. Some of the owners of the Chicago Bulls basketball team had called him up recently, looking to put money into one of his funds. Curiously, he discouraged them from doing so. "I told them I was too nervous about the market," he recalled. Taylor wouldn't say any more, but clearly he was feeling a lot of pressure. Sitting at his desk, he removed his designer glasses. The frames had left deep grooves on the soft, pale skin of his face, and his eyes were red. He looked older, almost forlorn, as if he had aged a few years since the summer. I noticed he had stopped talking as much about what the model said, as if tired of hearing it himself. "We're making a one-way bet against the dollar," Taylor began again, trancelike, starting to repeat himself. "Let's see if it works . . . I think it will work."

But it wasn't working. Two days later, the dollar enjoyed a surprisingly powerful rally after the unemployment rate came in at 4.4 percent, well below analyst forecasts and at a five-year low. That news dampened expectations for a rate cut anytime soon. When I reached Taylor by phone in Connecticut, where he was surveying some property for a separate business, he sounded a bit cranky. He was in a conspiratorial mood. With the midterm congressional elections a week away, he blamed the unexpected drop in the unemployment rate on the Bush administration monkeying around with data to boost the Republicans' sagging chances to retain Congress. "I'm trying to figure how much money we lost!" he bellowed. He wasn't backing off, though. FX Concepts sold more dollars that day against the euro and other European currencies, like the Swedish krona.

Then, just as the model said it would, the dollar began tumbling versus the euro and the pound. Despite repeated all-time highs in the Dow Industrials, the currency market was becoming more concerned about the U.S. economy and rates and was taking this fear out on the dollar. On January 2, 2007, Taylor strode into the office, beaming in a pink tailored shirt with tasteful gold-and-silver-crossed cuff links. FX Concepts's main fund managed to end the year with a 5 percent return, while its fund that trades primarily emerging market currencies chalked up an impressive 19 percent gain. Perhaps the firm's models have adapted to the new market trends after all.

Thanks to the dollar's big November and early December sell-off, the year-end push had worked. Now Taylor saw much more pain for the greenback in the year ahead. The stock market, he thought, was near a peak and would fall. The European and Japanese economies would pick up in 2007, and their interest rates would rise, while the U.S. economy faced a recession and rate cuts. There goes that yield advantage that had attracted foreign investors to the United States. His conviction was so strong that he gave the dollar a one-in-three chance of collapsing, a move he defines as tumbling 20 percent or more over a period of a few months. Such a scenario could rattle the U.S. financial markets, and with the dollar at the center of the global economy, it could have powerful effects on stocks and bonds worldwide.

"I think 2007 will be a very tough year for the dollar," Taylor said. Then he added mischievously: "But first, in January, I think the dollar will trick everyone and go up. That's what the model's saying." It was time to turn course on the $13 billion ship again and buy dollars. Time to walk as close as possible to the edge of the cliff, a sometimes lonely place, but one where the real money is made.

CHAPTER 2

Blowing Up the Money Factory

On a breezy summer day in 2005, Larry Felix boarded a taxi cab in Brooklyn and asked the driver to take him to the borough's public library. The New York native had spent the past twenty-three years working for the U.S. Treasury Department in Washington, D.C., and he wanted to meet with a friend from the old neighborhood. As the cab approached the curb of the library's majestic Grand Army Plaza branch, Felix handed over a $20 note. The driver stared hard at his passenger, then eyed the crumpled bill suspiciously. There had been a recent wave of counterfeit twenties circulating in this part of town, and the cabbie clearly didn't want to get stuck with phony money. But he knew what to do. The driver spent a few moments scrutinizing the bill's watermark, holding it up to the bright noon light that streamed through his window. "Even better," Felix suddenly piped up from the back seat, "check the number twenty in the lower-right-hand corner. It changes colors, from copper to green, when you turn it." The cabbie shot Felix a skeptical look—"Who *is* this guy?" it seemed to say. But then the driver turned the bill in his hands, as instructed, and began slowly nodding. Satisfied, he handed Felix his change and sped away to his next fare.

"If every merchant took that attitude, counterfeiting would be a lot lower," Felix told me, when I visited him in the fall of 2006 at his Washington office. He ought to know. As head of the Bureau of Engraving and Printing (BEP), Felix runs America's money factory—the only institution in the world authorized to print U.S. currency. With operations in the capital and in Fort Worth, Texas, the BEP has just one customer: the Federal Reserve. The bureau's printing presses run around the clock, five days a week (sometimes seven days a week), producing around 9 billion notes annually. Bureau employees load the notes into armored trucks to distribute them to the twelve regional Federal Reserve banks. They in turn send the new bills to commercial banks across the country and throughout the world. That's how those dollars ended up in your wallet.

Or, more likely, in foreign purses or billfolds. The U.S. government estimates that of the $760 billion worth of American currency in circulation, about two-thirds of those bills are changing hands internationally or are socked away overseas. The Federal Reserve also estimates that about 80 percent of the growth in the use of the dollar since the 1980s has been abroad.

For most of the twentieth century, the BEP was little more than the Fed's printing press—routinely cranking out, packaging, and delivering dollars. Over the past few years, however, the BEP's mandate has changed as radically as that of any government agency. The rise of the personal computer and color copiers has given birth to a new, more savvy breed of amateur counterfeiters, people who are able to produce at home better, more realistic facsimiles of the U.S. currency than ever before.

The professional counterfeiters continue to hone their craft. In recent years, the government in North Korea has emerged as the world's most notorious funny money maker. Kim Jong Il's regime uses the same intaglio press—employing top-of-the-line Swiss-manufacturing equipment available only to governments—and even managed to print currency on paper using the identical mix of three-quarters cotton, one-quarter linen found in real U.S. currency. This extraordinary dollar facsimile has been dubbed the Supernote by U.S. government officials. While much of the globe has focused on Pyongyang's frightening acquisition of nuclear technology, certain members of the U.S. State Department and National Security Council make their livings worrying about the counterfeit threat emanating from North Korea. These experts consider any attempt to destabilize the U.S. economy by sowing mistrust in the currency an act of war in its own right.

So in 1996, the BEP released a redesigned $100 bill—the first visible change to any note since 1928. The most obvious difference with the new bill was Ben Franklin's portrait, which was blown up to about four times its previous size. More important, there were a number of new security features that were introduced to foil counterfeiters: a watermark to the right of Franklin's portrait that can be seen from both sides when held up to the light, a thread that includes the words "USA 100" to the left of the portrait that glows red when put under ultraviolet light, and color-shifting ink that shifts from green to black on the 100 numeral in the lower-right-hand corner. (The BEP says Internet rumors of hidden owls and spiders on the currency are not true.)

These notes used the most sophisticated anti-counterfeiting technology the world had ever seen. But the bureau's work had only just begun. Over the following ten years, the BEP redesigned the $5, $10, $20, and $50 bills to include new security features. And now, to remain one step ahead of an increasingly confident band of domestic and international counterfeiters, the cycle begins again.

In 2008, the BEP is poised to release a new $5 bill and then a new $100 note—the mother of all currencies, the most widely used and highly coveted note in the world. Little has been made public yet about the new hundred, but Felix says it is likely to include a series of embedded micro lenses. This will allow images to move from side to side or up and down when the bills are tilted.

Between now and the new hundred's debut, the BEP, founded in 1874, itself is going through some of the most dramatic changes in its 133-year history. New equipment will enable it to print a greater amount of currency in order to meet global demand, and it will be able to print foreign currencies as well. The new printing presses will also allow the bureau to do something it hasn't done in seventy years: produce bills in different sizes for different denominations. This is something the BEP has been considering ever since a lawsuit was filed by the American Council of the Blind in 2002 to force the bureau to print bills that can be distinguished by the visually impaired. In November 2006, a federal judge ordered the BEP to redesign all bills so that blind people could easily identify notes of different denominations. The Treasury Department has appealed that decision.

"Everything you see is being changed," Felix tells me excitedly, motioning to the giant yellow printing presses rapidly spitting out sheets of $20 bills. "We are blowing up the factory!" Then he looks worried that that last comment may have sounded too glib. "This is our problem in a nutshell," he starts again, his voice lowered. "Make a currency as complex as humanly possible to manufacture but easy enough for the person on the street to recognize. Create more secure design changes, but still keep it uniquely American. And then do it billions and billions of times."

•   •   •

One can't pass through the (well-fortified) doors of the Bureau of Engraving and Printing without thinking about history. More specifically, about the history of American money. In the days before the American Revolution, the colonies used foreign currencies—the British pound, of course, but also the French franc and German mark, among others. The sight of the first U.S. mint for producing coins was in Philadelphia, the young country's capital at the time, built in an abandoned brewery, just a few blocks from George Washington's residence.

Up until the middle of the nineteenth century, hundreds of private and state banks issued thousands of their own currencies. But in 1861, Congress authorized the secretary of the treasury to issue paper currency to help fund the Union's Civil War campaign. The government lacked a facility to produce this currency, so it was outsourced to private firms. Then, in 1874, Congress created the Bureau of Engraving and Printing as the money-producing arm of the Treasury Department. It was around this time that the dollar received its nickname, the greenback, because of the green dye used to prevent reproduction. Counterfeiters then relied mostly on photographic copies, and their black-and-white film was not able to capture the greenback's colored hues.

After sharing quarters with the Treasury Department for a few years, the BEP got its own building in Washington, D.C., in 1880. Back then, the bureau was responsible for a lot more than printing dollars. It designed or produced currencies for countries like the Philippines, Cuba, and the Kingdom of Siam (now called Thailand). It churned out gold and silver certificates, Treasury notes, postage stamps, and even invitations to the president's inaugural ceremonies. By the turn of the century, the BEP and its many duties had outgrown its home. So in 1914, the staff moved into a stately neoclassical building between Fourteenth and Fifteenth Streets in the southwest section of the District of Columbia. The building is still used today, and some shameful remnants of earlier days can still be found. Visitors walking through its wide halls will notice, for instance, that two separate men's restrooms exist side by side: a legacy from the Jim Crow days when male workers of different races were assigned different bathrooms. In 1938, an annex was completed next door, and in 1991, the BEP expanded further with the opening of its Western Currency Facility in Fort Worth, Texas.

During the first few decades at the BEP's new building in Washington, the printing presses cranked out bills in denominations more commonly associated with the board game Monopoly. There were notes worth $500, $1,000, $5,000, and $10,000. Incredibly, there was even a $100,000 note, though it was used only for inter-bank transfers and was never distributed to the public. Since 1969, the $100 bill has been the largest note produced at the BEP. The $1 bill, the most widely used note within the United States, has an average life span of just twenty-two months. That compares with an average nine-year life of the $100 note.

With the euro printed in denominations of €200 and €500, some in the U.S. government wondered if these larger notes would enable the new European currency to steal some of the dollar's world market share. A few years ago, the House Banking Committee held hearings about reintroducing larger-denomination bills. "But the Secret Service strongly objected," Felix says. It is easier for their agents to track illegal activity, the BEP director explained, if the bad guys need bulky suitcases to transfer stacks of cash. "It's not like the movies make it out to be," Felix added. "You know, where crooks hand over a million dollars in an attaché case. The typical briefcase could hold, maybe, $400,000. The Secret Service has no interest in making that number bigger."

The BEP is a self-sufficient agency that doesn't go hat in hand to Congress to request money. Its business model is straightforward. The bureau charges the Federal Reserve around 5.7 cents for each note it produces and delivers. For the fiscal year 2005, the BEP took in revenue of $512 million. "We're like a private company," Felix told me. It's a private company with the capital's most voracious appetite for utilities and other resources: The BEP consumes eighteen tons of ink every day of operation, and it is also the capital's biggest user of water, steam, and electricity. All that energy goes into producing about 33 million notes with a face value of about $529 million every twenty-four hours.

Although people at the BEP design the bills and select the new security devices included in each new note, the treasury secretary has the final say on what any new bill will look like. As Thomas Ferguson, Felix's predecessor as BEP director, told me a couple of years ago as the bureau was starting to rethink the new $100 bill, "The only requirement is that Ben Franklin has to be on it somewhere. If the treasury secretary wants Elvis on the bill, I'd ask him if he wants the fat or thin one."

Few treasury secretaries bother to indulge this power; most are content to mug for the camera in the now-routine photo of the new head of Treasury signing his name to a bill. But Robert Rubin, treasury secretary from 1995 to 1999 under President Bill Clinton, took this particular role more seriously. When BEP officials showed him a mock-up of the new $20 bill about to be printed, Felix recalls, the treasury secretary frowned. To fit in new security features, the bill's designers had removed a circle that framed the portrait of Andrew Jackson. Rubin thought the bill looked classier with the circle, and he told the BEP to go back to the drawing board and design a new bill that included the old portrait frame. So they did, even though it added a few months to the time schedule to move new safety features around the circle so that everything could fit. "Rubin was very traditional," Felix says.

•   •   •

It's 9:00 A.M. on a rainy October morning and Felix
has assembled, inside the main conference room, the
eight heads of departments at the BEP. They include
Charlene Williams, who waves, via a large plasma video
screen, from the Fort Worth plant. The room is modestly decorated. On one wall is an oil portrait of Andrew
Jackson—the same one that is found on the $20 bill. A
bust of George Washington, in a regal pose that looks
more like Emperor Caesar than the first democratically
elected president, sits alone in a corner of the room. Most
of the walls are covered with only one thing: money.
Row after row of framed antique notes are displayed,
with a face value of hundreds of thousands of dollars.
Some are orange-tinged bills from the nineteenth century, and some $500- and $1,000-denomination notes
are almost lime green.

It's one of the first meetings of the BEP's new fiscal
year, one in which the BEP looks to radically change its
procedures. But at this gathering at least, there is no mention of "blowing up the factory." Instead, the talk turns
to more mundane troubleshooting. "We're making good
progress on ink adhesion," says Greg Boutin, an intense,
gaunt man with a long gray ponytail who is in charge of
new technologies. "No ink adhesion issues . . . We noticed the paper, when unwrapped, had creases. I'm thinking it's the paper, not the equipment."

Felix listens intently. He's leaning forward, his eyeglasses resting three-quarters of the way down the bridge
of his nose. Although he's been director for less than a
year, he seems at ease with everyone, and not just the executives at this meeting. Over the course of the week,
walking around with him in the BEP's main building and

the annex, Felix recognizes and calls out the names of an astonishing number of the bureau's 2,500 employees, from many of the 160 full-time police officers assigned to the buildings to the union workers operating the printing and engraving machines. While he has a commodious office that offers a prime view each spring of blooming cherry blossom trees near Washington's outdoor Mall, Felix seems to spend most of his time running around. He moves his muscular frame agilely as he navigates the various underground passageways between the bureau's two buildings, ducking away from a cart of equipment to his left, dodging workers carrying a six-foot-long tube to his right.

Felix has been with the BEP since 1992, after spending ten years in the Treasury department. His moustache is trim, and his closely cropped scalp of black hair is sprinkled with white specks. The forty-eight-year-old is the first African American director of the BEP. He was born in Port of Spain, Trinidad, and raised in the ethnically mixed neighborhood of Crown Heights, Brooklyn. After earning degrees in economics and political science at City University of New York, he did doctoral work in political economy at Columbia University before joining the banking world. He began with a stint marketing financial products at Irving Trust, reporting each day to an office at One Wall Street. "But I always wanted to work in government," he said. These days, he arrives each morning around 6:00 A.M. to check out the end of the night shift, which concludes an hour later. He won't go home for another twelve hours this day, and then he'll stay up late to help paint theatrical sets for his fifteen-year-old daughter's upcoming play. But despite his obvious energy, he's sworn off caffeine. Instead, he totes a bottle of water with him throughout the day.

Like many employees at the BEP, there is something in Felix's past that drew him to not only public service but to the arcane process of manufacturing money. As a child in Brooklyn, he says, his grandfather collected coins and paper currency. "I was the only grandkid who showed any interest in the hobby," he recalled. And while his focus in college was on international politics, his years at the BEP have sparked a powerful interest in U.S. history, especially the periods around the American Revolution and Civil War. The day we meet, he was in the middle of reading three books at once: one on Teddy Roosevelt's presidency, one on George Washington's military career, and one on Thomas Jefferson's leadership style.

•   •   •

American currency may be as sophisticated as any in the world, employing cutting-edge safety technologies and some hidden features that not even the shrewdest counterfeiters can discover. But the basic routine of engraving and printing bill after bill is amazingly similar today to the way it's been done for centuries. It remains an odd mix of slow, painfully detailed hand-craftsmanship followed by rapid mass output on the factory floor.

The BEP's thirteen engravers still use the same scalpels that were used in the eighteenth century to make tiny imprints in chromium-coated plates that provide the details in dollar bills. The talented engravers still must carve the notes' portraits, lettering, and all numerals in reverse, under lighted magnifying glasses, to produce the necessary mirror image for the plates. And if they slip or make even a minor mistake, the price is often the same as it was 200 years ago: trashing the plates and starting all over again from scratch, wasting months and months of work. Once the engravers are finished carving the plates for the front and back of the bills, metal sheets are indented with the engraving. The sheets are covered in great big blobs of greenish ink, and then BEP employees scrape off all excess ink. What's left behind settles into the small grooves on the plates. The plates are buffed with talcum powder to a brilliant shine.

Now, the BEP is ready to send special paper under the engraved plates. This paper, a unique blend of three-quarters cotton and one-quarter linen, comes from Crane & Co. The historic Dalton, Massachusetts, company has been in business since the eighteenth century. Among its list of blue-chip customers, Paul Revere once ordered Crane paper for use in the Colony of Massachusetts's banknotes, which helped finance the American Revolution. Crane has been a supplier to the BEP since 1879. Today, the world's most valuable paper is made from something almost as all-American as the dollar itself—blue jeans. Crane buys literally tons of scraps of discarded denim, removes the natural waxes and oils from the cotton, and bleaches it white. Then Crane workers add the security devices to their specialized pulp: red and blue fibers and a watermark. Finally, they add a coating to help the paper print well and then ship the sheets off to the BEP. Once there, the paper is in the hands of James Brent's crew.

"I can't look at a dollar bill without thinking, is it centered properly?" Brent tells me, chuckling to himself.

The sixteen-year BEP veteran is chief of the Office of Currency production. That means he oversees the entire production process of turning sheets of the cotton-linen paper into newly minted bills. Around 700 people work for him—nearly one-third of the entire bureau—and his group cranks out about 33 million notes a day, with a face value of about $529 million. Perhaps no one in the world is as intimate with the details of money production as Brent. In his office, he tells me that anytime he's given a bill, such as when he receives his change at a restaurant or withdraws a stack of twenties from an ATM, "I hold it up to the light and check it. Is the margin correct?"

As he speaks, the room shakes and I wonder briefly if Washington, D.C., ever experiences earthquakes. But Brent explains that the violent rumbling is only vibrations from a currency tank—a steel and glass box on wheels that holds 640,000 individual notes—being wheeled across the floor in the room directly above his office. "But before you see the room with the currency tanks," he says, "you should start by seeing the printing presses."

We ascend to the Section Nine printing area, where the three-week process of creating new dollar bills begins. It is a football-field-sized room with two large machines that look like stacked yellow port containers connected to conveyor belts. The room can barely contain them. These are intaglio presses, and each can produce up to 150,000 sheets, or 4.8 million individual notes, a day. They are forty feet long, fifteen feet high, and weigh ninety-five tons. The BEP building was constructed decades before anyone envisioned printing machines of this bulk and magnitude, and the intaglio presses just squeeze beneath the ceiling. In fact, Brent notes, workers had to remove entire sections of the wall just to fit pieces of the press inside the room for assembly. Railroad tracks on the floor were used to transport parts of the press from one side of the room to the other. Piecing it together took a full month.

Once assembled, the BEP's printing presses began to run nonstop, Monday through Friday, except during certain periods when they don't stop running at all. That's the case about a third of the time, Brent says. In 1999—when all government agencies and businesses took extra precautions in the event a Y2K bug struck on January 1, 2000—the BEP presses essentially never shut down all year long, producing a record 11.3 billion new notes. Sometimes, when he finds himself restless in the middle of the night, or if it's simply been a while since he's done an early morning spot check, Brent will get up from his suburban Virginia home and drive to the BEP to observe the nightshift in person.

As we enter the room, it sounds like a construction site. The giant presses clatter away at a decibel level just below that of a heavy metal concert. Signs everywhere in the room instruct workers to save their hearing by wearing earplugs, and most seem to comply. A Fox News broadcast blares at high volume to rise above the clatter. For the more than 250,000 annual visitors who make the BEP one of the capital's most popular attractions, this is where the tour begins. This day, a couple of dozen people are huddling on platforms about twelve feet above the workshop's floor, pressing their fingertips and noses against the glass walls and trying to sneak photos with cell phone cameras before they're scolded that any photography is prohibited. They watch as sheets of thirty-two bills are being printed on one side of the paper. Over the next three days, the sheets will be air dried. The notes are then printed on the other side, and then the sheets dry for three more days.

From the printing presses the sheets of bills are transported to a place known as the Vault. In this room, the climate is strictly controlled with a temperature of seventy-two degrees and a relative humidity of 50 percent. In here, the sheets of bills are stacked and then stamped with serial numbers and the seal of the Federal Reserve. Entering the Vault, you are hit immediately with a strong whiff of crisp paper and fresh ink. If there's such a thing as the smell of money, this must be it.

The Vault is a startling sight to behold. Square stacks of bills are scattered throughout the room like bushels of hay or desks in an overenrolled high school classroom. A woman in a purple vest kneads a large block of $1 bills as if lovingly giving them a massage, loosening the blocks of sheets stuck together so they can be more easily separated by the machines. In here, surrounded by more riches than Croesus possessed, the mind can't help but calculate the worth of each stack or bundle of dollars nearby. Brent smiles after I've totaled the value of twenties in a nearby currency tank ($12.8 million!), insisting that it's not long before most workers stop thinking so consciously about the value of the product around them. "After a few weeks," he assures me, "all you see is cotton and linen. We might as well be printing calendars."

Finally, we enter the packaging room. Only a limited number of BEP employees have access to this room, and I soon learn why. It's on the third floor of the BEP's main building and it's roughly the size of a small high school gymnasium. The lighting is soft, and the windows are tinted beige. Ten rows of double columns run through the room's center. It could be mistaken for one of thousands of different warehouses across the country except for one distinguishing feature: the money contained in this room.

Brent takes a cursory glance around him. "Hard to know what the value is of the notes in here," he says casually, "but it's billions and billions." It takes a little while for this to sink in. Whatever the exact total is, it's greater than the annual GDP of Tonga. Everywhere you look are orderly rows of bills, shrink-wrapped and stacked between two green plastic lids like giant dollar sandwiches. Nothing suggests the sort of security one would associate with a room containing an almost unfathomable amount of cash. The packaging room's two managers sit alone in their office, shuffling paper. A couple of forklifts lie idly. A stereo plays funk music that mingles with the buzz of packaging machines. The destruction of this building and all its currency could shake the U.S. economy, and Felix told me that the BEP was rumored to be one of the potential targets of the downed United Airlines jet in Pennsylvania on September 11. Whenever the level on the Terror Alert system rises above orange, Felix added, the BEP closes down to visitors.

Back in the packaging room, Brent picks up a brick of $100 notes—that's 4,000 bills stacked and shrink-wrapped—and hands it to me. It weighs nine pounds, and in your arms, it feels like you're holding a fire log. Then Brent picks up another brick of hundreds and puts that one on top of the first. I'm now holding $800,000 in cash in my arms. Two fire logs—so that's what holding that much money feels like.

The stacks of money won't stay here long. Some of them will be picked up this morning, sometime around 4:00 A.M., when an armored truck will arrive and take the new bills to Washington's National Airport, where they will be flown to one of the twelve regional Federal Reserve Banks. From there, the new notes will be transported to any of the 21,000 commercial banks, savings and loans, or credit unions across the country and around the globe.

*   *   *

HAVE YOU EVER BEEN SO CLOSE AND YET SO FAR AWAY? reads a sign hanging in the middle of the main BEP printing room. It is meant to be a slyly humorous reminder that, in fact, the bureau is not printing calendars but a product that makes the world go round. The Depression-era thief Willie Sutton, when asked why he robbed banks, is said to have answered, "Because that's where the money is." But did it ever cross Sutton's mind to wonder where the banks got *their* money? Would the BEP's money factory not be the ultimate bank robber's prize?

According to Felix, no outsider has ever attempted a heist at the Bureau of Engraving and Printing. The BEP's security measures are certainly a deterrent. Any visitor has to pass by an armed guard's booth. Once inside, there's a staff of 160 police officers. Every bag and personal item is searched thoroughly upon entering and leaving the bureau. There are metal detectors at all entrances and security checkpoints in every room where money is being made or stored. The biggest deterrent of all, Felix argues, is that every new note is accounted for by a corresponding serial number. The moment a robbery is detected, the BEP would send out an all-points bulletin to every major financial institution and law enforcement agency in the world, alerting them to the theft and preventing any robber from stowing the new cash anywhere respectable.

Inside jobs at the BEP are another story. Since 1993, there have been eleven reported thefts by BEP employees, totaling nearly $2 million. In nine of these cases, the thieves were convicted; in two, no suspects were identified. Some of these thefts came even after extraordinary precautions were put in place in response to a minor rash of thefts in the mid-1990s that drew harsh criticism from Treasury Secretary Rubin.

In addition to the BEP's nearly 1,000 internal cameras and the many sensitive areas in the building that require special approval to enter, the bureau runs extensive checks on all potential employees. They are screened for any criminal background and subject to extensive credit-history checks. BEP officials even visit homes in person, where they interview a prospective hire's neighbors and look inside their houses to see if people who will be surrounded by towers of freshly minted cash "are . . . living beyond their means," as Felix put it delicately. Even after they are hired, BEP employees are given random drug tests, and every five years they are reassessed, with full credit checks and return visits to their homes. Employee movements within the workday are limited, too. For a long time, staff couldn't even leave the building for lunch.

But all the checks, probes, and disincentives will

never change the fact that to be surrounded by billions of dollars is to be immersed in wicked temptation: BEP employees are like kids in the ultimate candy store; day after day, and year after year, they can look, and they can touch. But they cannot indulge.

The tastiest treats, it seems—the ones that have drawn the most illicit attention from workers—are the millions of notes earmarked for destruction each year. About 3 percent of the more than 8 billion new bills the BEP produces annually are deemed flawed in some way. At one point during the three-week process, the ink may have smeared or perhaps the paper crinkled. Of course, such imperfections will result almost immediately after the notes are released into circulation. Yet the BEP insists that only immaculate notes leave its vaults.

That means some 30 million bills each year are targeted for destruction. Unlike the pristine notes that are sent to the Federal Reserve banks for broad distribution, these flawed notes are not as closely cataloged, and in many cases are removed before they have serial numbers. The doomed notes, known internally as "mutts," are rejected by machines that can spot any minor imperfection. They are then bundled and sent to a separate office within the BEP, where they sit for a few days to a week as they await their final destiny of shredding, burning, or baling. "Notes aimed for destruction are our biggest vulnerability," Felix said. "How can you tell if they are destroyed?"

Donald Stokes Jr., for one, figured you probably couldn't. An employee at the BEP's Forth Worth plant since 1991, Stokes was known as a verifier, a position that accounts for all currency produced. In 2005, the thirty-nine-year-old pleaded guilty to transporting stolen cash across state lines. He received a sentence of forty-one months in federal prison.

Government officials said Stokes had pilfered more than $700,000 in these flawed bills. He had methodically stuffed sheets of $20 and $50 bills intended for destruction into his pockets and passed through security undetected, authorities said. At least three times a month over an eight-year period, Stokes sneaked five to ten sheets into the men's room, stuffed them under his shirt, and then walked right out again. A Secret Service agent testified in court that Stokes told agents he had become disgruntled and began his illicit spree in 1997. In October 2004, the BEP discovered that $5,000 had gone missing. Stokes was among the suspects, and in March of 2005, agents searched his home and found wads of cash stuffed into one of his jackets.

That same day, Stokes took off. Borrowing a relative's identification card, the former BEP verifier fled by car through Arkansas, Oklahoma, Colorado, Nevada, and New Mexico. He took breaks from his fugitive run to enjoy the Grand Canyon and Death Valley, according to court testimony. Authorities finally tracked Stokes down the next month in Oklahoma City, cornering him after a wild car chase at speeds up to 90 miles an hour. In Stokes's automobile, agents found about $80,000 in cash; around $29,000 of that was identified as money from the BEP plant, while Stokes claimed to have won the remainder gambling, an agent testified.

Less than a year later, the BEP's Washington office would prove to be just as vulnerable. David Faison confessed to stealing twenty-one sheets of $100 bills that he tried to launder through casinos. His job at the bureau was to distribute large sheets of the specialized paper that is used to print dollars. This gave Faison access to the restricted area where new bills are printed. He was caught after casinos in Atlantic City, West Virginia, and Delaware noticed that Faison had been passing $100 bills that lacked both the Federal Reserve seal and serial numbers. Video cameras in the casinos showed that the perpetrator would insert his stolen bills into a slot machine, play for a bit, and then cash out, taking with him the casino's real bills. Authorities found nine sheets of $100 bills at Faison's home and another $14,500 in stolen bills at the casinos. Faison, who hid the stolen property inside Christmas wrapping paper at his Largo, Maryland, home, pleaded guilty to stealing counterfeiting materials. In February 2007, he was sentenced to nine months in prison.

But the most infamous bandit in the history of the BEP was one of the last people at the bureau anyone would have expected. In 1989, a precocious twenty-six-year-old named Robert P. Schmitt Jr. was put in charge of an elite team to create the new security thread that would be part of the redesigned $100 bills. This marked one of the BEP's first efforts to foil counterfeiting in the personal computer age, and the security thread was widely viewed as a big success in the United States and abroad. As for Schmitt, he was considered "an up-and-coming star on the management staff," said the BEP's spokesperson, Norma Opgrand. That was until June 1994, when he was arrested for stealing $1.7 million in freshly minted $100 bills.

This time, there was nothing as cinematic as a cross-state high-speed pursuit or high-rolling casino bets to launder money. The BEP engineer's theft was much more methodical, and Schmitt showed the sort of patience that none of the other thieves appeared to possess. Indeed, his elaborate plan made all previous attempts to steal from the BEP look about as sophisticated as a street mugging.

A graduate of Carnegie Mellon University, Schmitt was paid $66,890 for his job at the bureau. Though he lived with his mother in suburban Maryland, Schmitt supported a girlfriend and two children. Schmitt smuggled the $100 notes out of the BEP's second-floor vault using special keys held by him and only five other top-level employees. Today, all packages and bags leaving the BEP must first pass through an x-ray machine. But back then, Schmitt was able to smuggle the notes out of the building by concealing them in a zippered compartment of his briefcase that security guards failed to examine.

That was just the first phase of his plan. The bills he stole were left over from a test run of bills that were ultimately ordered for destruction. These test bills looked identical to the genuine article, even down to the use of real serial numbers. Schmitt's genius was to hold on to those bills for four years—until a month after real bills with the same serial numbers were sent by the Federal Reserve into circulation. Consequently, his notes' appearance in a bank wouldn't trigger any alarms. After all, Schmitt's test bills had serial numbers that were now legitimately found in public circulation. Schmitt also knew that a bank is required by law to report to government authorities any cash deposit of $10,000 or more. So he made a series of deposits at eight different branches of Annapolis Bank and Trust, each at sums just below that limit.

He also bought things. Like land. Schmitt purchased a Chesapeake Bay three-bedroom home—complete with a swimming pool, hot tub, and two garages—for $400,000 in 1994. He put one-quarter of that amount down in cash. He paid cash for a $126,000 condominium in nearby Ocean City. Neighbors said Schmitt's mother told them she had come into a large and unexpected inheritance and that she lent the money to her son for the purchase of the new homes. He was negotiating for a third home, this one in the District of Columbia for around $250,000, when he was caught.

His scheme finally fell apart when Annapolis bank officials became suspicious of his regular deposits of crisp $100 bills that always came in just below the legal reporting limit of $10,000. When tallied up, these deposits came to $213,787 over a period of just two months. The day government agents finally busted Schmitt—the same day another man under suspicion, O. J. Simpson, fled from Los Angeles police in a white Ford Bronco—they found $500,000 stuffed inside a safety deposit box and another $650,000 tucked away in his Nissan 300 ZX sports car.

Once caught, Schmitt confessed, blaming his transgression on what his lawyers called a "diminished capacity" that resulted from his heavy use of Prozac. By the time of his trial in U.S. District Court, he told the judge he had switched to Xanax. "It just relaxes me, to the best of my knowledge," Schmitt explained to the court, according to the *Washington Post*. A few months later, in March 1995, he was sentenced to twenty-seven months in prison.

•   •   •

While the Bureau of Engraving and Printing focuses most of its efforts on churning out billions of new notes a year, it also quietly excels in a lesser-known role: It is the world's dollar redeemer of last resort. The BEP will accept just about any torn, chewed on, digested, discolored, blackened, or shrunken dollar bill, no matter how badly it smells or how toxic its appearance. The bureau receives on average 200 to 300 envelopes or packages or moldy containers of mutilated currency each day. As long as at least 51 percent of the bill remains and can be verified as genuine, the BEP will, free of charge, refund the owner for the currency's full face value.

In 2006, the BEP handled 20,000 such cases and sent out checks worth $66 million—some to places as far away as China, Poland, and Uruguay. BEP officials say they are the only government organization in the world that performs such a function. So meticulous is the staff that they have been known to spend up to two years analyzing a single package of gnarled currency.

"We don't care if it was in a fire, buried underground, water damaged," says Roscoe Ferguson, a fifty-four-year-old supervisor at the BEP's Mutilated Currency Division. "Maybe your dog ate it. Came out the other end. Clean it up a bit. We'll take care of it."

The Federal Reserve is in charge of disposing worn-out currency that commercial banks send it in exchange for fresh new bills. About 4 million of these old dollars are shredded and compressed into small bricks each day. They are then usually sent to landfills or packaged for the occasional souvenir for visitors to the Fed.

But it's the BEP's Mutilated Currency Division that has reimbursed individuals for their partially destroyed bills since 1862. New employees spend six months in training, during which they learn how to reconstruct a note with the same painstaking precision a Swiss watchmaker spends assembling springs and coils to tell time. Trainees are also taught by the Secret Service to be able to spot counterfeit notes.

"We teach them how recognize the colors, the texture, the security designs of a note," says Lorraine Robinson, who runs this division of twenty people and has been working with mutilated currency since 1974. "We teach them what color of black burned money turns."

The very fact that such a department exists is testimony to the unusual durability of the U.S. currency and its unique cotton-linen composition. The BEP claims a bill's fibers are so strong that one could fold a note over and over on itself up to 4,000 times before it will tear.

Nevertheless, Ferguson has seen a lot of unusual things happen to currency during his sixteen years at the bureau. He is one of a handful of elite specialists authorized to handle the toughest cases, known as Level Five. A former Federal Bureau of Investigations agent ("I left because they kept pushing me to get married") and a former Washington, D.C., cop, Ferguson (still a bachelor) has been with the bureau's Mutilated Currency Division since 1990.

If a fool and his money are soon parted, it's Ferguson's job to see that many of them are somehow reunited. He says the group once received a bag full of green strips from a man whose enraged wife had run much of his life's savings through a paper shredder.

A specialist at the Mutilated Currency Division spent two months piecing the ripped notes together like a jigsaw puzzle until every strip fit. The bureau sent the man a check for $30,000. Several years earlier, an Iowa farmer dropped his wallet in a pasture and one of his cows turned it into a snack. The farmer slaughtered the cow, cut out its stomach, and mailed the contents to the BEP. A couple of months later, he received a check for $600. In 2001, a Florida man attempted to dry his soggy bills by placing them in a microwave oven. "It wasn't a good idea," he wrote to The Miami Herald. "They caught fire." He received a check for $700.

The twenty people at the division work in close quarters, in a few rows of cubicles that could be mistaken for most any other suburban office, except for the equipment they each stock: cleansers, large magnifying glasses, knitting needles, knives, tweezers, scalpels, and many cans of Lysol. The job requires tremendous patience and the steady hand of a surgeon, as employees sit hunched over well-illuminated desks, gingerly pulling apart mutilated bills that have been reduced to the consistency of damp tissue paper. Robinson says they lose many seemingly good candidates during the first two years— people who find the work distasteful. But those who make it those initial two years tend to stick around for life, she adds.

Most in the Mutilated Currency Division are fans of crossword puzzles and mystery novels, and their work offers something of the intrigue that you might find in a detective story or a Law & Order episode. For instance, a short-sighted bank robber once sent in bills that were stained with a pink dye. Instead of a check from the BEP, he was rewarded with a knock on his front door by the police. The Mutilated Currency Division was able to detect the bills' serial numbers. In a separate case, the largest redemption ever was in 1978 for the sum of $2.5 million. An armored car had been damaged after an explosion in downtown New York City.

One October afternoon in 2006, Ferguson told me about receiving several wallets from victims of Hurricane Katrina. "The odor was horrific," he recalls, wrinkling his nose. But he was still glad people sent in those wallets. He says the satisfaction he gets from reuniting folks with their life's savings makes even the unsanitary aspects of the job worthwhile. "You're helping people who think they've lost it all and are so grateful," he says. "That's what I like. I've received hundreds of phone calls and letters. I'm an instant member of the family afterwards."

Indeed, after any major disaster or cruel act of nature, the BEP spreads the word about its mutilated currency service through a number of channels: the local police and fire department, the Federal Emergency Management Agency (FEMA), and the Homeland Security Department. The massive destruction from the collapse of the World Trade Center towers on September 11 turned much of everything into ash. But Robinson says the BEP still received about 150 claims related to that day, primarily from people with security deposit boxes located in banks with vaults in the basements of the towers. One man kept a wad of bills in a safety deposit box in one of the destroyed towers. A few months later, he recovered a box of the charred bills that had shrunk to a quarter of their normal size. He sent it in. The BEP cut him a check for $400,000.

•   •   •

In many ways, 1989 was a historic year. The fall of
the Berlin Wall signaled the end of Eastern European so-
cialism, and the subsequent capitulations by authoritar-
ian regimes from Prague to Bucharest marked the end of
a Cold War that had divided the world for nearly five
decades. That year would mark the start of a new era for
the world of currency, too. And like the conclusion to
the Cold War, it would signal potentially profound effects for the United States.

The collapse of the Iron Curtain made hundreds of
millions of people instantly eligible and eager to participate in the capitalist world. Since most currencies printed
by deposed regimes were suddenly suspect even by locals, many Eastern Europeans turned to the dollar as the
best way to store and protect their savings. It was, after
all, the legal tender of a conquering nation—the currency of triumphant Cold Warriors whose economic
system had won the war of ideas.

To meet this burgeoning overseas demand, the BEP
was compelled to crank up the presses, especially for the
popular $100 note. "It really grew as the international
currency in the nineties," Thomas Ferguson, the BEP's
director at the end of that decade, told me. In 1991—the
final year of the Soviet Union's existence—about 1.8 billion individual $100 bills circulated the globe. As new
countries entered the capitalist world, demand for America's largest denomination note soared. With the dollar
no longer tied to gold, the U.S. government faced few
constraints in printing more dollars to satisfy the booming
new global demand. By 1996, when the first redesigned

bill hit the streets, there were 2.5 billion $100 notes in circulation. Today, that figure exceeds 4.5 billion, with about three-quarters of those $100 bills held or circulating abroad.

The year 1989 saw another groundbreaking development for the dollar, but this was a more troubling one. That December, a money handler at the Central Bank of the Philippines found something odd about one of the $100 notes he was counting, even though the bill passed the usual tests of authenticity. The central bank passed on this peculiar note to the U.S. Secret Service. The Secret Service determined that the note was a counterfeit after running it through ultraviolet lights and examining it under a microscope. But it was no ordinary fake. The paper consisted of the same cotton-linen blend used by the BEP, so the fake note felt astonishingly like a real dollar. The quality of the engraving also exceeded that of any other counterfeit bills the agents had ever seen. The Secret Service had just come across its first Supernote.

This discovery meant that several decades of quiet on the counterfeiting front had come to an end, and the lazy days of the BEP merely serving as the government's passive printing press had come to a screeching halt. A new evolution in technology and the burgeoning use of the dollar worldwide mean that the bureau was now called on to fight forgers big and small, Michael Lambert, assistant director in the division of reserve bank operations and payment systems at the Federal Reserve, told me. For the first time in seven decades, the twenty-two-year veteran of the Fed added, "we realized that U.S. currency is going to have to change."

In one corner, there was a growing legion of amateurs whose home computers and cutting-edge color printers could produce crude fakes—counterfeits that were close enough to fool absent-minded shop owners or bank tellers. In another corner, there was now a highly skilled international counterfeiting group, a syndicate that appeared to have ties to a government and was thus able to get its hands on the same intaglio presses used at the BEP. The bureau's crucial new task was to develop a currency that could not easily be replicated by either of these groups and to distribute the new bills globally before the world at large ever started to doubt their dollars' authenticity. No less than the dollar's credibility was at stake.

.   .   .

Counterfeit dollars have been around as long as the dollar itself. The trade became particularly rampant during the period known as the Free Banking Era, which began in 1837 after President Andrew Jackson let the charter for America's central bank, the Second Bank of the United States, expire. State-chartered banks assumed many of the roles formerly held by the central bank, including the printing of paper money. Each state bank— there were more than 700 of them at the time, printing thousands of different kinds of bills—could issue its own notes, each with its own peculiar design and eccentricities. This cornucopia of currencies, and the lack of any national standards or consistent designs, made the climate ripe for counterfeiters and nearly impossible for the average citizen to glean what dollars were real and which were fakes. How could citizens know for sure when state banks adorned their notes with everything from beauty pageant candidates to Santa Claus?

Newsletters offering detailed accounts of the latest counterfeit notes became crucial tools of the trade for shopkeepers and bartenders. One such publication, "A Counterfeit Detector and Bank Note List," spelled out in amazing detail the sheer variety of frauds that business owners faced daily. In one 1839 issue, the booklet described notes from more than 250 banks that were regularly counterfeited, another fifty-four bills that were worthless (but continued to circulate even though the issuing banks had failed), and twenty notes from banks that had never existed at all. "It was hard to know anymore what a dollar ought to look like, and the farther a dollar traveled from the bank that issued it, the more gingerly it was treated by people who could not be expected to recognize the note or even the bank, let alone assess its reputation," Jason Goodwin wrote in *Greenback: The Almighty Dollar and the Invention of America.* The Fed estimates that counterfeits represented as much as one-third of all bills in circulation during the Free Banking Era. This freewheeling period came to a close in 1863 with the National Banking Act, which established a national currency. Moreover, the Secret Service was created two years later—the same day President Lincoln was shot—for the purpose of preventing any counterfeiting of America's new national currency.

Forgers persisted, albeit at a much lower level. During most of the twentieth century, counterfeiters used giant printing presses to ply their trade. This equipment's bulk, expense, immobility, and difficulty in operation served as built-in disincentives to potential entrants to the field. But the introduction of the home computer and color printer—sophisticated, easy-to-use equipment that could fit into a briefcase—suddenly empowered the amateur counterfeiter. In 1995, the year before the BEP released the first of the redesigned bills that included the new $100 note, the American public lost $2.4 million because of color-copier counterfeits, according to the Federal Reserve.

That figure is a tiny fraction of the hundreds of billions' worth of dollars circulating inside the United States at the time, and it looks even tinier compared with the country's $14 trillion a year gross domestic product today. But it nevertheless raised concerns that a new counterfeiting era loomed. In response, the BEP and central banks from around the world organized a private meeting with all the major manufacturers of color copiers to get the private sector involved in fighting forgery. "The international group successfully negotiated a technical solution, which was implemented in color copier equipment, to recognize bank notes and prevent them from being copied," Lambert and Kristin D. Stanton of the Federal Reserve Board's Division of Reserve Bank Operations and Payment Systems wrote in a Fed publication in 2001. The partnership produced the desired results; by 2000, the amount of money lost to counterfeits from color copiers had fallen to just $1 million, according to the Federal Reserve. The Secret Service estimates that only about 1/100 of a percent of all dollars in circulation are counterfeit, and overall, the Fed suggested that any counterfeiting problem within the United States was well under control.

* * *

But if the U.S. government had begun to clamp down on the home-grown lay counterfeiters, a growing professional breed abroad offered a more complicated challenge. Aside from the fact that the international counterfeiters tend to be better financed and more sophisticated, a number were associated with foreign governments.

There's a long, checkered history of governments producing phony currency either to raise funds or, more frequently, to undermine an enemy. This tactic goes back at least as far as 1470, when the Milanese Duke Galeazzo Sforza tried to disrupt the rival Venetian economy by printing fake Venetian currency. Counterfeiting as a tool of war really took off in the twentieth century. After the Germans suffered a stinging defeat in the Battle of Britain in 1940, the Nazis tried a different tack. They produced counterfeit notes of various denominations, worth about 150 million British pounds. Dubbed Operation Kruger, after the SS officer who devised the plan, the notes were designed by well-known counterfeiters and were produced by prisoners of Nazi concentration camps. If they couldn't bomb the British into surrendering, the German military reasoned, they would inflict pain through another channel. Their hope was that word of the widespread circulation of bogus British currency would undermine confidence in the pound and eventually cause havoc to the U.K. economy. Amazingly, for a government that murdered millions of its own people, some German officers initially opposed Operation Kruger, arguing that it represented an unnecessary attack on a civilian population.

The Nazi plan failed to dent the British economy, but that didn't discourage London from hatching its own counterfeit schemes during the war, most in far-off places like Malaysia, Burma, and China. The British even fought back with the production of some phony Reichsmarks of their own to give the Germans a taste of the same medicine.

In later decades, the United States joined the counterfeiting game, printing bogus Cuban pesos in an effort to topple Fidel Castro. The U.S. government also cranked out fake North Vietnamese dong, hoping to destabilize that economy during the Vietnam War.

More recently, it's been foreign entities who have been suspected of trying to harm the U.S. economy by printing funny money—from unfriendly governments to stateless terrorist organizations. Increasingly, Washington has come to view counterfeiting as a national security issue. Michael Green, a former member of the U.S. National Security Council, told *The New York Times Magazine* that counterfeiting constituted an "act of war," while another senior administration official told the magazine that counterfeiting represented "a threat to the American people."

Not long after the Secret Service discovered the Supernote from the Philippines, other examples of these state-of-the-art fakes began popping up in distant corners of the globe, from Greece to Macau, China (then under Portuguese administration). Still, the American government was uncertain about the notes' creator. Florida congressman Bill McCollum, chairman of the House

Taskforce on Terrorism and Unconventional Warfare, issued a 1992 report that fingered Iran as the culprit. The
committee suggested that it might not be long before billions of Supernotes were circulating around the world.
But the theory of Tehran as a hotbed of counterfeit dollars proved short-lived. Instead, government officials
began to focus farther east, on North Korea.

American intelligence on the North Korean leader
Kim Jong Il depicts a man with a long-held interest in
counterfeiting. Accounts of North Korean defectors suggest that the "Dear Leader" (as he is known in his country)
saw printing foreign currencies as a way for Pyongyang to
finance its various operations and as a means of waging
economic war on a sworn enemy. On several occasions,
North Korean diplomats had been caught in foreign countries with Supernotes. By the start of the new century,
Washington defined a Supernote as an exceptional counterfeit made exclusively in North Korea. In 2003, the U.S.
State Department created the Illicit Activities Initiative, a
division of the department developed specifically to inves-
tigate covert activities in North Korea.

Perhaps the dollar's best protective device against
counterfeiters is the color-shifting ink found in all new
bills—the feature that Larry Felix pointed out to his
Brooklyn cab driver. In 1996, the United States purchased the exclusive rights from the Swiss manufacturer
SICPA for the green-to-black ink that is found in the
$100 note. Not long after, Pyongyang put in a large
order to the same company for color-shifting ink, too.
On the face of it, it was an odd request. The SICPA ink is
very expensive compared with regular printing ink, and
North Korea is one of the poorest countries in the world.

Moreover, its currency holds no appeal to counterfeiters. But American suspicions soon rose: The North Koreans requested ink that shifts colors from green to magenta, which was the nearest combination available to what the United States had ordered, according to a U.S. government official who spoke with me only on the condition of anonymity.

Up until the North Korean interest in counterfeiting became clear, Colombian drug traffickers had been considered the top counterfeiting threat, and in terms of pure volume, the Colombian fakes still vastly outnumber the North Korean paper. But Washington now suspects North Korea of producing Supernotes of such fine quality that even government experts have a hard time distinguishing them from the real thing. Some U.S. government officials even hypothesized that the minor, hard-to-spot defects in the Supernotes were actually intentional—put there by the North Koreans so that *they* could distinguish the phony bills from the genuine article. In fact, in some details, the Supernotes even appear to be of superior quality to genuine dollars. For instance, the hands on the clock tower of Independence Hall, which are found on the back of the $100 bill, actually looked sharper on some of the seized counterfeit notes than on ones produced at the BEP.

In his office, Felix looks slightly embarrassed upon hearing this, but he explains that government forgers produce far fewer notes than the BEP does. Thus, in an odd way, they can be more exacting in their standards, just as Henry Higgins was able to tutor cockney Eliza Doolittle to speak with the most refined of English accents. "Counterfeiters always worry they'll get caught," he says. "The first clue to me is when something is too crisp, too perfect."

Despite the high quality of their product, even the Supernote producers face long odds in ever causing an economic disruption in the United States. Yet counterfeiters have succeeded in sparking momentary crises of confidence in the dollar abroad. In some small economies—like Taiwan, for example—that regularly use the dollar, an outbreak of counterfeit paper has caused banks and shops to turn away dollars for fear of accepting worthless fakes. The most recent case was in Peru, where in May 2005 police arrested two men and confiscated around $4 million worth of counterfeit notes—and some fake euros to boot. Many of the notes were already packed in boxes to be shipped to Ecuador, Peruvian authorities told the media. The phony notes in Peru weren't detected until the Federal Reserve tested some of the notes from Peruvian commercial banks that had accounts with the Fed branch in Miami, says Lambert.

The Fed can spot a Supernote in an instant: The central bank has high-speed processing equipment that searches for certain covert features in U.S. currency that are not visible to the naked eye and that even the most sophisticated counterfeiters cannot duplicate. After the Fed discovered the Supernotes, Lambert flew out to Lima, Peru, as well as to other South American countries like Chile and Bolivia, to help central banks there sort out the counterfeit notes. For a few months in Peru, Lambert says, some commercial banks often rejected $100 bills with certain serial numbers that were suspected of being fakes. That made Lima business in general more wary of dealing in $100 bills until the end of that summer, when confidence returned that most of the Supernotes had been detected and removed from circulation.

The U.S. government has seized about $48 million worth of Supernotes since the first one was detected in 1989. Still, as far as he knows, Felix has seen a Supernote only on one occasion, while on a business trip to Panama, a country that has used the dollar as its main currency since 1904. For someone who has dedicated much of his adult life to scrutinizing U.S. currency, he was amazed at how difficult it was, even after several minutes of examination, to spot any difference from the real product. "It had the thread and the watermark," he recalls. "Only the crinkled feel was different."

.   .   .

The transition stage when newly designed bills are introduced is considered the most vulnerable period for fraud. "When is the best time to pass a counterfeit note?" Felix quizzed me back in his Washington office. "When new bills are hitting the market. That's when there is the most confusion. And that's why you need to educate people."

Toward that end, the BEP has spent $30 million to promote public awareness, at home and abroad, of the look and safety features in its new bills. The bureau set up toll-free hotlines across the globe and sent representatives around the world to discuss the new designs and anti-counterfeiting properties. When the beige-tinted new $10 bill was introduced in 2005, the BEP circulated posters and pamphlets in twenty-four languages, including Uzbek and Vietnamese.

Although the United States has said repeatedly that old bills will never be recalled and will always be worth exactly the same as the new ones, these transition periods are often accompanied by a dip in the use of the dollar abroad. In 1995, a year in which new bills were introduced, the growth in the overseas use of the dollar rose a meager 3 percent, after averaging 8.5 percent annually over the previous two decades. Fed officials attributed the temporary slowdown to mistaken fears that the old bills would lose their value. Even these days, newly minted dollars are deemed to be worth more than older ones in many countries. *The Wall Street Journal* reported in 2006 that a souvenir store in Moscow refused to accept $20 bills for Russian nesting dolls or premium vodka if they were signed by Treasury Secretary Robert Rubin. They were considered too old. Likewise the Stella Matutian Lodge in Goma, Democratic Republic of Congo, is happy to accept $100 bills signed by recent Treasury Secretary John W. Snow and even those autographed by his predecessor Paul H. O'Neill. But the O'Neill bills are worth only $90 at the lodge.

As the BEP prepares for the release in 2008 of the first redesigned $100 bill since 1996, Felix acknowledges that counterfeiters have managed to alter the bureau's schedule. Originally, the bill was slated for a 2007 launch. But the proliferation of counterfeiters who were bleaching and then transforming the $5 note to look like the $100 bill encouraged the BEP to redesign the $5 bill first and disrupt this popular scheme. Felix and his colleagues at the BEP are otherwise pretty mum about the look and new features of next year's $100 bill—other than to boast it will be the hardest note to counterfeit ever. "But don't forget," Felix adds quickly, "there's no such thing as a counterfeit-proof note. With the right equipment, you can copy anything. The idea is to make the costs of reproduction so high that you draw the attention of law enforcement."

CHAPTER 3

More Sound Than the Pound,
and Good as Gold

The hot summer of 1971 would leave its mark on U.S. history in startling ways. Two American astronauts drove the Lunar Rover across a powdery gray landscape to become the first space travelers to explore the mountains of the moon. *The New York Times* published excerpts of the Pentagon Papers, exposing secret government deliberations to escalate the Vietnam War. In upstate New York, 1,281 inmates seized control of the Attica maximum security penitentiary in one of the deadliest ever prison riots. And one steamy August weekend, President Nixon and fifteen advisors met in the rustic mountain retreat of Camp David to devise a plan for tackling the country's economic woes. The result was dubbed the New Economic Policy and, in the words of economic historian and author Daniel Yergin, it entailed "a momentous step in the history of international economics."

Ever the political animal, Nixon was hesitant to unveil this master plan on primetime television if it meant preempting the popular western *Bonanza* and aggravating its legion of fans. But advisors prevailed upon him to make an announcement before the financial markets reopened on

Monday. So, on the night of Sunday, August 15, 1971, the thirty-seventh president of the United States appeared on all three television networks to announce to the world that the dollar was abandoning the gold standard.

"We had little choice," Paul Volcker, a key player in that landmark decision, recalled during an interview at his Manhattan office in 2007. "We were running out of gold. There was a threat of a run on the dollar. Eventually there would be a crisis."

Best known as head of the Federal Reserve from 1979 to 1987, Volcker was a high-ranking official at the Treasury Department when the United States ended the gold standard that, in one form or another, had provided the backbone of international finance for more than a century. It is Volcker's fate that he will forever lie in the shadow of his more famous successor as Fed chairman, Alan Greenspan, who presided over one of the greatest economic booms and stock market bull runs (though he also manned the controls during the bursting of the tech bubble). But there may be no single individual more directly responsible for the dollar's ascendancy in the final decades of the twentieth century than Paul Volcker.

As the Treasury's undersecretary for international monetary affairs, Volcker was perhaps the person most instrumental in pressing for the United States to break the historic Bretton Woods agreement. This treatise placed the dollar at the nexus of the world's financial system by linking the U.S. currency to gold and all other major currencies to the dollar. The decision to end the gold standard was in part a practical necessity. Under Bretton Woods, all dollars held by foreign central banks were considered "good as gold" and could be swapped

for American supply of the precious metal at the central
bank's request. By that summer of 1971, foreign countries held three times as much in dollars as the United
States government had in gold; the U.S. government realized it was in no position to honor every request to
trade dollars for gold—or even to honor many requests
if they came at once.

Abandoning the trusty gold standard thrust the
global economy into the great unknown. The first several years were rough ones for the dollar, which steadily
lost value against the yen and most major European currencies. Yet jettisoning Bretton Woods also liberated the
dollar, setting the stage for its wider use in the 1990s. As
Federal Reserve chairman, Volcker would staunch the
long slide in the dollar's credibility by pushing up interest rates to unimaginable levels to cure rampant inflation.
His actions would throw the country deep into recession, causing a collapse in lending and the highest unemployment rate in forty years. But the harsh medicine
would ultimately help heal the sick economy. That the
dollar remains today the world's most important currency is in no small part thanks to Volcker's push to end
the gold standard and his determination to bail out the
dollar afterward.

Many economists and politicians saw the end of gold
convertibility principally as a sign of American weakness. Few recognized that it was also an opportunity to
spread the dollar's influence even wider—that if gold at
first helped legitimize the dollar as an international currency, by the 1970s it was threatening to undermine it.
Only when dollars could be printed and valued separately from gold could the currency's true potential be

realized. "There was great irony," Volcker told me, referring to the post-gold-standard era when more dollars circulated throughout the world than ever before. "People were more willing to hold dollars that weren't backed by gold than they ever were willing to hold dollars that were backed by gold."

Today's powerful wave of globalization owes much to the dollar's freedom from gold and to the world's eagerness to hold the U.S. currency anyway. That freedom brought about new advantages and new dangers for the world economy, particularly for the United States. Before we examine those advantages and dangers, it's useful to see how the dollar climbed to its privileged perch and what distinguished it from all internationally used currencies that preceded it.

•   •   •

Near-universal demand for the greenback reached a fevered pitch at the end of the Cold War in the 1990s, as the Eastern bloc embraced the dollar as if it were a passport to the capitalist world they were suddenly free to enter. But the concept of an international currency is hardly a new one. It's been around since before Christ. Over the previous 2,500 years, there have been more than a dozen currencies that were regularly accepted as a form of payment beyond their own borders. Such currencies include the Greek drachma, which changed hands regularly before 500 B.C.; the liang, a round Chinese coin marked by a square hole in its center; Indian silver coins; the Islamic dinar of the Middle Ages; the Venetian ducato of the Italian Renaissance period; the

Dutch gilder of the seventeenth century; the British pound sterling from the eighteenth century to the mid-twentieth century; and, finally, the U.S. dollar.

Today, the euro is the most recent—some would say the first serious—potential challenger to the dollar's rule. The International Monetary Fund, in a 2006 report, indicated the benefits of an "international money," which is something that most economists have long agreed on. The widespread use of a single currency cuts foreign exchange transaction costs and boosts international trade and investment.

A global currency serves at least three basic roles for the world economy:

- as a medium of exchange for people and companies in different countries to agree on a price in a currency that is acceptable to both parties
- as a store of value, or a way to hold savings without fear of a severe loss in value over time
- as a unit of account, or as a means for measuring the worth of an object or a service

As explorers began to travel the world, people started to talk of a day when there would be one currency that was easy to carry and would be accepted at all borders. Exactly when the idea of a single currency originated is a matter of some dispute. Robert Mundell, an economist at Columbia University and a Nobel Prize winner who advised the European Union on the creation of the euro, points to the Italian count Gasparo Scaruffi. In the sixteenth century, the count proposed a world currency that he dubbed the altifono, which is said to mean "true light." Morrison Bonpasse, founder and president of the Single Global Currency Association, a nonprofit group devoted to the creation of a new, Esperanto-like world currency, suggests that by "world" Scaruffi must have meant no more than Western Europe. Bonpasse believes that the British philosopher John Stuart Mill was the original voice for a utopian planet where every nation transacted in the same coin. Bonpasse points to *Principles of Political Economy: with some of their applications to social philosophy* (1848), in which Mill wrote, "Let us suppose that all countries had the same currency, as in the progress of political improvement they one day will have."

The British government was a step ahead of Mill. With steam power enabling the rapid production of a paper currency that was difficult to counterfeit, central banks grew increasingly comfortable with holding interest-bearing claims on foreign currencies, rather than just gold. In this budding era of international currency, London was eager to serve as the world's banker. Britain relied on its colonial outposts to internationalize the pound, establishing banking branches in the colonies while colonial banks in turn opened offices in London. The pound's holders stretched from North America to the Far East and down to South Asia, where it became India's legal tender in 1899.

The British used the privilege of empire to impose the pound on their colonies. The pound, however, was uniquely qualified to serve as the world's main currency in many other ways. Britain was the leading trading and creditor nation, and London was the world's leading financial center. Just as crucially, until 1871, the pound was the only major currency with an unconditional guarantee of convertibility to gold. For much of the

nineteenth century, the French central bank, for instance, often refused other governments' requests to
convert its francs to gold, offering the disappointed foreign officials depreciated silver instead.

By the early twentieth century, the pound had established itself as a currency used in most every corner of
the globe. Yet curiously, it was largely absent from its
own backyard. To Britain's great frustration, the franc
and the mark dominated central bank holdings in conti-
nental Europe (despite central bank grumblings about
inconsistent gold convertibility), where France and Germany's influence dominated southern and eastern Europe. The pound was a distant third. Even one of
sterling's great competitive advantages—its guaranteed
convertibility to gold—proved to be less than ironclad in
the 1930s. With the onset of the Great Depression, England's economy was in shambles. Unemployment stood
at 20 percent, its budget deficit was ballooning, and
global confidence in the pound was eroding. Defending
the pound would have required raising interest rates to
attract foreign capital, but such a move would have almost certainly plunged England deeper into recession by
making it more costly for consumers and businesses to
borrow to fund any new projects or purchases. When the
Bank of England instead opted to reduce interest rates in
an effort to stimulate the country's moribund economy,
foreign governments began to question the stability of
sterling as they rarely had before. The Bank of France
and other central banks accelerated their demands to
trade in sterling for gold. Fearing a run on its dwindling
bullion supply, Britain reluctantly suspended its gold
convertibility in 1931.

By then, a new currency had started circulating around Europe anyway. This currency came from a restless new emerging power that was gradually learning to exert its authority and to use its own currency to make inroads in the continent that the British Empire never did.

•   •   •

When the calendar turned to 1900, America's economic might was becoming increasingly clear. Europeans stopped debating in pubs and cafés about which rapidly developing country would become the next economic power of the twentieth century. Those who had argued that Argentina would exceed the United States soon realized they had bet on the wrong horse. By the turn of that century, the United States was the world's second-largest exporter. It was a leading producer of all sorts of manufactured goods and raw materials. It boasted a healthy balance-of-payments surplus. Yet, for all its economic muscle, the United States lacked a crucial element of global influence that each of the major European economic powers enjoyed: international use of its currency.

At the end of 1899, the British pound accounted for nearly two-thirds of official foreign exchange assets held by central banks around the world. The franc and mark accounted for about another 15 percent each, with other currencies making up the remainder. The pound, which had been the world economy's primary currency for international trade throughout the nineteenth century, faced growing challenges in that role from other European currencies. The dollar was scarcely used outside of North America. "The United

States was the only major trading country whose currency did not function as an international currency," wrote J. Lawrence Broz, a financial historian at the University of California, San Diego.

What stood in the dollar's way? For a country to enjoy international use of its currency, it has to fulfill at least two important criteria: the nation must have one currency, and one currency only, that is used for all its domestic transactions; and it needs a central bank to serve as a "lender of last resort" that would support the currency and give confidence to foreign banks that used it. Washington had already cleared one hurdle in the 1860s with the passage of the National Banking Acts, which established a single currency and created a system of national banks that helped finance the Union's costs of fighting the Civil War. But the other hurdle had yet to be cleared. America had no central bank.

For most of its history, the United States had viewed central banks—as its people viewed most any symbol of centralized authority—with a skepticism that bordered on open hostility. Alexander Hamilton, one of the nation's founding fathers, was naturally sympathetic to this sentiment. But as George Washington's secretary of the Treasury, he also recognized that the young country needed financial stability if it was to survive. Hamilton devised the First Bank of the United States to develop a national currency and to serve as a lender of last resort. The bank was established in Philadelphia, but moved to the nation's capital in 1791. However, Hamilton never won over his congressional critics, many of whom opposed his central bank for political reasons. They argued that this institution was not mandated in the U.S. Constitution, and, in

1811, Congress voted not to renew the bank's charter. After the Supreme Court ruled that the bank was indeed legal, Congress rechartered the Second Bank of the United States in 1816. The new bank was constructed grandly in the style of a Greek temple. But Democratic opponents were more mistrustful than ever. This time, they accused the bank of fraud and corruption, leading President Andrew Jackson in 1832 to veto a renewal of the bank's charter. It expired four years later.

Jackson's speech on the July day on which he wielded his veto pen made it clear that, whatever corruption may have existed ("suspicions are entertained and charges are made of gross abuse and violations of its charter," he said cryptically), Jackson viewed the bank as unacceptably cozy with foreign interests: "More than eight millions [*sic*] of the stock of this bank are held by foreigners. . . . Should the stock of the bank principally pass into the hands of the subjects of a foreign country, and we should unfortunately become involved in a war with that country, what would be our condition?" (It was the sort of nativist refrain that nearly eighty years later the framers of America's third attempt at a central bank, the Federal Reserve, would hear again and again. But on the third attempt to establish the bank, they finally resolved it.)

Over the next few decades, the nation's banking system was divided along regional and state lines without a central authority to unite it. During this volatile period, the federal government had little control over standard banking and lending practices, and state-chartered banks issued their own notes as currency. It wasn't until the Civil War broke out in 1861 that the government took steps to reunite the nation's banking system again. The

Banking Acts of 1863 to 1865 created a system of national banks. These laws gave the federal government—as opposed to the individual state governments—regulatory control over the nation's banks and created a new market for Treasury bonds, since Washington required all banks to secure their currency issuance with U.S. government debt securities. While the acts were blatantly political, created to fund the Union's war effort, they also had the palliative effect of cleaning up America's banking mess. Under Washington's watchful eye, national banks had stricter capital reserve requirements than did state banks, and some of the riskier loans, such as those for property speculation, would now be limited.

Yet, for all the helpful reform measures, nineteenth-century America was still what economists would classify today as an emerging market. The nation's financial institutions were immature and unreliable, political corruption was rampant, and the country was undergoing a rapid transformation from an agrarian-led economy to an industrial powerhouse. This evolution would propel the U.S. economy to the top ranks of the world: By 1890, with mining and manufacturing now surpassing agriculture as the main engine of U.S. economic growth, America generated more output per person than most of Europe. But it would be a wrenching transition marked by dramatic boom and bust cycles that the government— lacking the infrastructure and, most of all, a central bank—was ill-equipped to smooth out.

The financial panics and bank runs that had become regular ordeals during the pre–Civil War period were not about to go away. Financial crises occurred in 1873, 1884, 1890, 1893, and 1907. In between, the U.S. economy suffered, by some estimates, as many as two dozen less-severe panics. Indeed, Americans of the late nineteenth and early twentieth century could count themselves lucky if they made it through the year without having their lives disrupted by some sort of major bank failure or stock market crash. During these panics, many people found the bank teller window rudely slammed in their face when they tried to withdraw their life's savings. But banks had little alternative. Federal deposit insurance did not come into existence until 1933, and private insurance for bank deposits was hard to find. This uncertainty also punished businesses, which often had to scrap new expansion plans when corporate loans were recalled or were not rolled over.

The Panic of 1907, though overshadowed by the Great Depression a little more than two decades later, was perhaps the worst financial crisis the young nation had yet endured. A stock market crash delivered the first blow, and eventually the unemployment rate soared to 20 percent. Thousands of banks collapsed as millions sat by helplessly, watching their life's savings evaporate. With politicians unsure of what to do to fix the mess, the Treasury secretary turned to the famed and controversial banker John Pierpont "J. P." Morgan. The government put $25 million at the financier's disposal, and Morgan assumed the role of America's central banker, offering temporary loans to major banks while letting others fail.

Morgan called a meeting of the nation's trust company presidents at his lavish New York City apartment, where he prodded them to contribute to a bank rescue fund. The barrel-chested financier locked trust company presidents inside his ornate library and would not let them out until they opened their checkbooks. While the trust presidents argued and deliberated, Morgan played solitaire in an adjoining room, rejecting proposal after proposal until the bankers reached one he could approve.

When the panic subsided, powerful forces in the government and the private sector began to coalesce around the idea of reform. Wall Street and Washington concluded that the United States could no longer tolerate the repeated threat of financial meltdowns. Many of these banking crises occurred in the autumn, during the harvest season, when demand for currency intensified because farmers often insisted on cash payments. With many people simultaneously withdrawing cash from banks for these seasonal food purchases, bank reserves could fall quickly, leaving them more vulnerable to runs. During these periods, many banks also raised interest rates in an effort to attract more deposits, thus boosting their reserves to meet this temporary demand for currency. The sudden rise in interest rates, however, frequently resulted in an equally sudden slowdown in economic activity that heightened the chances of recession.

Despite widespread distrust for bankers and New York's financial elite, greater still was the fear of what might have happened if there had not been an aging bank tycoon to step in as the nation's reluctant savior. The role of central banker—a lender of last resort—would have to be made official. A central bank, as financial author and historian Ron Chernow noted, "could mobilize scattered reserves during crises, much as a fire department could pool water." But during these repeated panics, America's 22,000 banks typically worried only about extinguishing the fire in their own marbled lobbies.

They hoarded precious reserves at times of crisis, as to be expected. But by preventing their weaker peers from getting access to much-needed capital, the banks' behavior had the unintended consequence of aggravating the overall instability of the country's banking system. So, even many relatively healthy banks ended up tainted by association when there was a panic.

This crucial period in the history of American finance would see the birth of the Federal Reserve and the dawn of a new era of relative financial stability. It marked the evolution of the U.S. financial system from a haphazard state of risky circumstances dependent on the actions—good and bad—of individuals to a more formal structure backed by the federal government. One of the most important and immediate beneficiaries of this would be the dollar.

•   •   •

While all Americans would certainly be better off with a central bank that would steady the financial system and reduce the frequency of panics, New York's banking elite had an added incentive. For the dollar to be taken seriously as a store or value or means of exchange abroad, the United States needed a central bank that could stand as a lender of last resort and provide the anchor for the broader and deeper financial markets already found in Europe. "International usage of the U.S. currency was the special inducement for bankers to lobby for the Federal Reserve," Broz wrote. That inducement, Broz continued, went straight to the bottom line: International use of the dollar meant extra commissions and other fees that would follow from the many foreign companies they anticipated converting their currencies into dollars. Moreover, Broz added, "the use of the [dollar] as a reserve asset brings large inflows of funds into the central money market, thereby increasing demand for banker services." National City Bank, for instance, estimated that prior to 1914, English banks earned $150 million annually in commissions from financing American exports.

Still, these bankers were well aware that any of their overt lobbying would likely doom the creation of a central bank. Many Americans were deeply suspicious of Morgan (even after his crucial role in the financial bailout) and the other moneymakers on Wall Street. The last thing the financiers wanted was for a new central bank to be perceived as the personal playpen for top-hatted bankers. With that in mind, Wall Street proceeded with uncharacteristic discretion. In 1910, a group of New York bankers quietly met at a seaside resort off the coast of Georgia known as the Jekyll Island Club (one of Morgan's favorite retreats). Nosy reporters asking questions were told it was only a duck-hunting trip. In reality, they were there to begin drafting legislation that would serve as the foundation for what would become the Federal Reserve Act of 1913.

The result of this "duck hunting" excursion would become known as the Aldrich Plan, named after U.S. senator Nelson W. Aldrich of Rhode Island (a direct descendant of Rhode Island founder Roger Williams). Aldrich was a stern believer that the 1907 panic made plain the need for a central bank, and he would become the Washington politician most associated with the Federal Reserve's creation. His brush-style moustache, thinning white hair, and banker blue suits bestowed on him a passing resemblance to Morgan, and his daughter's marriage to John D. Rockefeller Jr. would tie him directly to an even more financially powerful family. Many decades later, his grandson, Nelson Aldrich Rockefeller, a renowned businessman and philanthropist, would become governor of New York and later Gerald Ford's vice president.

Senator Aldrich attended the financiers' secret hunting session alongside an all-star roster of bankers and money managers that included J. P. Morgan's partner Harry Davison and Frank Vanderlip, president of First National City Bank, the precursor to today's financial behemoth Citigroup Inc. But the most consequential guest at Jekyll Island was an introverted European named Paul Warburg, who, having never shot a bird in his life, had to borrow a rifle to play along with the charade. Warburg was the head of the investment firm Kuhn, Loeb & Co., but at the Jekyll Island gathering, he became the grand designer of the Federal Reserve.

A scion of the German-Jewish clan that was one of Germany's leading banking families (until the Nazis stripped them of the business), Warburg was a thin and sickly child, but he showed early signs of creativity and intelligence, reciting poetry before his second birthday. As a young man, excused from military service for health reasons, his affluent family sent him on an extensive world tour, where he recorded—in verse—his memories of India, China, Japan, Egypt, and, finally, the United States. Warburg was then trained in the intricacies of the family business, European banking. Upon his arrival in New York, he was astounded to find that the United

States, with its powerful economy and its growing importance to world commerce, could have such an underdeveloped financial system. Warburg complained incredulously that it was "at about the same point that had been reached by Europe at the time of the Medicis."

Yet modernizing this antiquated banking system could not mean simply aping the European structure already in place. The United States remained, as ever, distrustful of centralized authority—of Washington politicians and perhaps even more so of the moneyed tycoons in New York. Critics in America's heartland considered a central bank a foreign import that they had hoped was dead and buried. To overcome this nativisim, Warburg devised a clever compromise plan for a uniquely American central bank (and, perhaps too coincidentally, chose this moment to file papers for American citizenry). To disperse power, there would be a system of regional banks, each accountable to separate boards. But a national board of commercial bankers would coordinate the regional banks' actions. The regional banks would be empowered to make emergency loans to any private bank that might need them, thus stifling a potential crisis at the source before the public could catch wind of an individual bank failure that might erode confidence more broadly. The regional banks would also have the power to create money, so that currency would be plentiful during traditional periods of scarcity, such as the autumnal demands for farmers' goods.

Once the central bank's blueprint was drafted, it had to be sold to the public. The genius of the bankers' sales plan was to promote the Federal Reserve Act as a "public good"—emphasizing that a lender of last resort would safeguard the nation from another painful wave of bank runs and market meltdowns. Of course, there was much truth to this claim. But for the plotters on Jekyll Island, the ulterior motive was to profit from the international-ization of the dollar. That could not happen without a central bank to improve confidence in the U.S. financial system. Warburg was selling the central bank one way to the general public, Broz maintains, and another to the members of the banking community, playing the strongest card in each case: "Although financial reform was couched in terms of the national interest, Warburg explicitly tied it to improving the international position of the dollar. In so doing, he gave the New York banking community private incentives to assume leadership of the reform effort."

Over the following months, the financiers under-took an aggressive and well-funded lobbying campaign to push the legislation through a Congress that often showed populist leanings. The bankers created the National Citizens' League for the Promotion of Sound Banking, a public relations organization that, in War-burg's words, would "carry on an active campaign of education and propaganda for monetary reform." The league published and circulated 15,000 copies of a primer called *Banking Reform*, which today would be called *Central Banking for Dummies*. The financiers targeted the press with a twice-monthly journal, circulation of 25,000, that was sent to newspaper editors. They tried to influence lawmakers by sponsoring letter-writing campaigns to Congress and by hiring speakers to spread the word at various interest-group meetings.

After some congressional wrangling, lawmakers passed

the Federal Reserve Act. The bill established a network of regional reserve banks that would issue shares held by private banks in those regions. The actions of the regional banks were to be guided by a Federal Reserve Board, whose members would be appointed by the president. It was a system closely aligned with the one Warburg had envisioned as a concession to the population's—and, by extension, Congress's—distrust of a central banking authority. In December 1913, President Wilson signed the bill into law. Shortly after, the president appointed Paul Warburg as a member of the Federal Reserve's first board.

* * *

While the New York financiers were ambivalent about provisions in the bill the president finally signed into law, they should have been elated. Just as the National Citizens' League for the Promotion of Sound Banking maintained, the U.S. financial system was noticeably more stable in the years that followed the creation of the Fed. Although the economy was brought to its knees by the financial crisis of 1929 that disrupted the world, the smaller crises and panics that characterized the U.S. economy began to fade. The "public good" that Warburg tirelessly championed as the underlying rationale for a central bank seemed to be borne out.

What had to be even more pleasing to Warburg and the other financiers was that with a central bank in place, international use of the dollar began to take off. For the first time, New York began to compete with London as a global banking center. By 1916—a mere three years after the Federal Reserve Act—the greenback was on its way to challenging the British pound as the world's most-used currency. The dollar was now used as the means of payment for trade between the United States and the rest of the world, a role previously reserved for the pound. Increasingly, the American currency was being used in trade among Europe and Latin America and the Far East. "The United States emerged as a nascent 'world banker,'" Broz wrote of the years that led up to the Roaring Twenties. "America's halting, tentative first steps as financial 'hegemon' in global affairs dates from this period."

Though they couldn't have grasped the significance at the time, these New York financiers had created another "public good"—one that would prove to be equally as important as smoothing out business cycles or limiting panics. By laying the foundation for the dollar's global role, the banking tycoons provided great benefits to future Americans—especially those living in the latter half of the twentieth century. No currency had ever played quite the role the dollar was destined to assume. For Washington, a global financial system fueled by the dollar would bring lower government borrowing costs through the ability to sell Treasury bonds at lower rates. It would enable corporate America to acquire foreign companies at marked-down prices. For American citizens, the global use of the dollar would mean cheaper financing on everything from automobiles to home mortgages—not to mention cheaper travel costs abroad.

By the end of World War I, the dollar was poised to take on the pound sterling for global dominance. Even as the Federal Reserve served as the lender of last resort (in effect, giving foreigners confidence that when exporting or importing products in dollars, there was an institution to back up these transactions on behalf of American commercial banks), other events conspired to further spread the dollar's prominence. Loans made by New York banks to the Allied nations broadened the dollar's circulation in Europe. Undeterred by the fighting, many U.S. financial institutions opened European branches during the war years. Britain's economy, overstretched by war costs and maintaining the empire, looked increasingly wobbly. Other potential rivals, meanwhile, frowned on the internationalization of their currencies. Germany viewed overseas use of the mark as a threat to its ability to control inflation, so the government imposed capital controls to discourage its use abroad. Japanese officials took similar measures.

Central banks across the Atlantic also began to hold dollar reserves for the first time around World War I. In 1928, the year before the stock market crash, major central banks held around $600 million in dollar holdings, compared with about $2.6 billion in other currencies. This amount would shrink considerably in the 1930s, when the worldwide Depression would lead central banks to shift most of their holdings to gold (the United States and the United Kingdom both ended the practice of converting their currencies to a fixed gold rate at the start of the decade, though the United States resumed the practice in 1934).

By the end of the Second World War, the dollar had emerged victorious. The greenback towered over all other currencies like none before it, perhaps the most conspicuous sign of American might and influence. Economic dominance of the world had not been seen of this magnitude before and is perhaps unlikely to be seen again. In part, this reflected the fact that the U.S. economy emerged stronger from the war while Japan and the European powers took years to heal from their battle wounds. In 1945, the United States accounted for about half the world's industrial production and—with a powerful central bank—boasted the largest financial markets. The world's new Goliath was also a treasure trove of natural resources: It produced half the world's coal and two-thirds of the world's oil.

The dollar's role at the center of the world financial system would be made official in 1944 in the town of Bretton Woods, New Hampshire. There, at the scenic Mount Washington Hotel, an agreement was hammered out among 730 delegates from forty-four nations. After the disastrous 1930s, when trade barriers and currency controls led to a breakdown of international trade, the leading powers aimed to create a system that would allow investment capital to flow easily across borders. The summit resulted in a compromise between two competing plans—one from the U.S. Treasury and one from John Maynard Keynes, the famed British economist. Keynes proposed creating a new world currency system that would issue a new international reserve asset, known as bancor, that could be used as a supplement to gold. This plan allowed a substitute "paper gold" and gave the system some protection from relying on a relatively scarce precious metal.

But as the conquering power—one with more than three-quarters of the world's gold reserves in its possession—America had other plans. In the past, major currencies had been fixed to gold. Now the Bretton Woods architects, led by U.S. Treasury official Harry

Dexter White, negotiated a plan that placed the dollar at the core. The greenback would be fixed to gold at a rate of $35 an ounce, and all other currencies would be arranged at fixed rates to the dollar. The International Monetary Fund (IMF) was also created at Bretton Woods. Among other duties, the IMF was put in charge of deciding when and if a country could change its fixed rate against the dollar. For its part, Washington agreed to convert foreign central bank dollar holdings into gold upon request.

As the currency of the world's newly minted superpower, the dollar's supremacy was not merely unchallenged—it was unprecedented. It was the currency of the biggest economy and the currency with the greatest purchasing power. Further, the dollar alone was backed by gold. The financial system laid out by the Bretton Woods agreement established the dollar as the lynchpin of the global monetary system. Never in the 2,500 years of international currency use had the world's major nations signed a document that officially enshrined one currency as the leader; never before had the world's powers formally agreed that there would be just one currency among which all other currencies would be measured. It was a major coup for the United States, among its greatest spoils of victory on the World War II battlefields.

•   •   •

Bretton Woods made it official: The dollar was now the world's currency. This privileged position was endorsed by all the major nations of the free world (the Soviet Union sent a representative to the New Hampshire summit, but ultimately declined to sign the agreement).

Over the next two decades, the dollar's place at the axis of the world's financial system seemed assured. By the 1960s, dollars accounted for some 60 percent of all central bank foreign reserves, an amount that was double that of its closest rival, the British pound. A decade later, nearly 85 percent of all foreign reserves were held in dollars.

Moreover, an increasing amount of international trade relied on the U.S. currency. In the Far East, for instance, most countries used the dollar not only when doing business with firms or customers in the United States. It was also the primary currency in any transactions among governments themselves. This represented a break from the past, when Pacific Rim countries had alternatively used the pound and Japanese yen as the main reserve and trade currency. "When China trades with Korea, or Thailand with Malaysia, all the transactions are in dollars," Ronald I. McKinnon, a professor of international economics at Stanford University, wrote. "Japan is the only Asian country that uses its own currency to invoice some of its trade. Even here, almost half of Japan's exports and three-quarters of its imports are in dollars." The currency's prestige even became a useful part of America's Cold War strategy. But none of that meant the dollar's dominance was guaranteed to last.

The new postwar monetary system faced two potential constraints. For starters, the United States guaranteed that central banks could, at any time, cash in all of their dollars for gold. In the 1940s, there was still enough gold in the world to cover this promise, and U.S. vaults held most of it. But as Eichengreen wrote, "In a rapidly growing world, it was only a matter of time before the gold scarcity would resurface, precipitating a crisis." Gold discoveries in western Australia and South Africa added to the global supply, but clearly the global economy—fueled by growing numbers of dollars—was expanding faster than new gold was being mined. This likely meant some mismatch down the line between foreign reserve dollar holdings and America's ability to exchange it for gold.

Of course, as long as foreigners were content to hold dollars instead of gold, there would be little cause for concern. And for a while this was the case. Western Europe's central banks were happy to hoard greenbacks, which had lower transaction costs than gold and earned them interest. The United States, meanwhile, was glad to pay that interest if it contributed to the economic reconstruction of its Cold War allies. From 1948 to 1954, Washington gave $17 billion to sixteen countries in Western Europe as part of the Marshall Plan, also known as the European Recovery Program, to rebuild the devastated European economies. By offering grants and favorable trade conditions to Western Europe, Washington was betting that revitalizing these economies (and Japan's) would ultimately benefit the United States. It would, Washington officials reasoned, generate overseas demand for U.S. products and create new outposts for corporate America's expansion abroad. And as tensions mounted with the Soviet Union, Western Europe's economic recovery would also make the region less vulnerable to Soviet influence.

Yet this massive flow of dollars abroad resulted in a ballooning deficit in the U.S. balance of payments (essentially the difference in all economic transactions between one country and the rest of the world). "The dollar's unique role in world trade and reserve creation meant that to a certain degree a deficit in the American balance of payments was desirable and even necessary for the international economy," Francis J. Gavin, assistant professor at the Lyndon B. Johnson School of Public Affairs at the University of Texas, Austin, wrote. "But as American dollar liabilities—created by the yearly payments deficit—increased, confidence in the gold convertibility of the dollar fell."

Simply put, U.S. officials began to worry that ever-widening deficits would cause European allies to doubt America's ability to exchange all those greenbacks for gold. If that ever happened, something akin to a global bank run could develop, where each of the European governments would demand gold for its dollars. The United States would be unable to honor all those requests simultaneously. That could spark a collapse not only of the dollar but of the global financial system.

These concerns surfaced as early as 1958, during the Eisenhower administration. From then through 1961, the United States lost $5.4 billion in gold, converting the precious metal to dollars at a rate that surely would have exhausted the U.S. supply by the end of the decade. President Kennedy told his aides that the two things that worried him the most were nuclear weapons and the rising balance of payments deficit. His administration undertook new policies to stem the flow of gold. Kennedy instructed the Treasury Department to intervene in the currency market to stabilize the dollar, and he pushed a change in the tax system meant to encourage exports and cut the deficit. Such efforts paid off, as central bank requests to convert dollars to gold leveled off.

It proved to be a temporary respite. By Lyndon B. Johnson's second term in the White House, the U.S. economy was feeling the pinch of its Cold War commitments. Although the Marshall Plan largesse had ended, America was funding an escalating war in Vietnam while continuing to foot the bill for a large military presence in West Germany that was considered necessary to deter the Soviets from invading. At the same time, LBJ had committed billions to his new Great Society program, which covered a variety of new policies from student aid and low-income housing loans to Medicare and Medicaid.

Despite Johnson's commitment to these plans, he and others in the administration fretted that the costs of their programs would bloat the budget and balance of payments deficit, weakening confidence in the dollar and potentially sparking gold withdrawals. To head this off, the United States undertook creative measures never anticipated by the authors of Bretton Woods. Under strong pressure from Washington, West Germany agreed to hold its dollars and not request any gold. France was less accommodating. "The United States is not capable of balancing its budget," French president de Gaulle railed against the superpower to Alain Peyrefitte, France's minister of information. "It allows itself to have enormous debts. Since the dollar is the reference currency everywhere, it can use others to suffer the effects of its poor management. It exports its inflation all over the world. This is not acceptable. This cannot last." De Gaulle did what he could to end it by converting billions of dollars to gold. He believed that if France converted enough of its dollars, other nations would fear a run on the U.S. supply and be forced to follow with requests of their own.

De Gaulle was also among the loudest to complain that the dollar system offered an unfair advantage to

American companies. Despite the high balance of payments deficit, the dollar enjoyed an artificially high value that enabled American investors to scoop up European companies at cut-rate prices—prompting de Gaulle to charge that France was "being submerged by monsters such as General Motors and IBM."

LBJ countered by preparing a leaner budgetary plan that he hoped would reduce the deficit, prop up confidence in the dollar, and fend off gold redemptions. In a more curious departure, the administration proposed, in effect, a new world currency, Special Drawing Rights, or SDRs. Johnson saw this as a supplement to gold that would be allocated by the IMF to countries based on their gold and dollar reserves. While SDRs were meant as a store of value similar to dollars or bullion that could be swapped among nations, they would not be convertible on demand into gold or dollars.

This so-called paper gold never caught on. At the end of LBJ's presidency, U.S. policymakers began plans to move the monetary system from fixed rates to one where currencies could trade, albeit confined to narrow bands, against each other. "The world supply of gold is insufficient to make the present system workable," Johnson said. Washington was forced to print more and more dollars to pay for the accelerating costs of the Vietnam War. This led to greater inflation, and the U.S. ability to convert dollars to gold became increasingly strained.

With the SDR strategy a nonstarter, Washington tried a different tack under newly elected President Nixon: playing the bully. The administration's goal was to convince its European allies, more from blatant arm-twisting

than persuasive rhetoric, to revalue their currencies against
the dollar to help boost America's export position and close
its yawning balance of payments deficit. The chief arm-
twister was Nixon's treasury secretary, a blunt-talking
Texan and LBJ protégé, John B. Connally. The secretary's
reputation for tough battles stretched back at least as far as
1963, when as governor of Texas he rode alongside
Kennedy in the open limousine on the day Kennedy was
assassinated. Connally was shot himself that day (a bullet
passed through him), but he would fully recover, switch al-
legiances to the Republican Party, and launch a successful
Washington career of his own. As head of Treasury, he was
adamant that the United States not take any steps to close
a balance of payments deficit if they carried any risks of
slowing the economy. Rather, he would pressure foreign heads of state to adjust their currencies against the
dollar. The tough-talking Texan suggested to a delegation of Europeans that they would just have to find a
way to revalue their currencies against the dollar if they
expected the United States to continue its military support. The dollar, he famously told them, is "our currency, but your problem."

The bully pulpit approach bought some time. France
and West Germany both agreed to alter their currencies'
value versus the greenback, and there was a period of
calm during which the United States pushed for greater
exchange-rate flexibility to protect its gold supply. Yet
the Europeans felt they had been pushed far enough, and
despite the temporary assistance from the currency reval-
uations, the American payments deficit began to bloat
again and eat away confidence in the greenback. By 1970,

America's gold coverage had slipped dramatically to a mere 22 percent of the dollars held in central banks abroad, down from recent levels of more than 50 percent.

An end to a landmark system that had been in place since 1944 seemed near. The House Subcommittee on International Exchange and Payments released a report in early August 1971 in which it was concluded that the "dollar is overvalued." The solution to the widening deficits that resulted from this overvalued currency, the report continued, was to change the exchange rate system. Barely a week later, President Nixon followed that policy prescription and took the dollar off the gold standard, suspending the right of central banks to convert all their dollars to bullion.

With one signature, he torpedoed the historic agreement made at Bretton Woods that had helped to rebuild the Western world. It was replaced by the Smithsonian Agreement, under which the dollar was devalued: Instead of $35 for an ounce of gold, it would be $38 for that ounce, and the value of gold could strengthen or weaken against the dollar within a narrow trading band. From here, it was only a matter of time until the dollar's value versus gold would plunge while the balance of payments deficit widened further. By 1972, gold was valued at $70.30, more than double the price set in 1944. The following year, the last of the trading limitations were scrapped. Even then, the dollar was still the most widely used and important currency the world had ever known. But it was about to face new challenges.

•   •   •

The front page of *The Wall Street Journal* called Nixon's surprise decision in 1971 to completely close the gold window a "stunning and sweeping" action. Economists predicted that the dollar would fall in value against the European currencies. As momentous as the decision to abandon the gold standard was, it still took a few years before the event was properly stamped into the American consciousness. "If historians searched for the precise date on which America's singular dominance of the world's economy ended, they might settle on August 15, 1971," wrote William Greider in his 1987 bestseller *Secrets of the Temple: How the Federal Reserve Runs the Country*.

Yet, if many observers recognized the potential for decline with the end of the gold standard, most failed to grasp that there was also a flipside of opportunity. The world's most important currency was about to be permanently untethered from gold, silver, or any other tangible asset that historically served as collateral for paper currencies. Instead, the dollar would be backed by something much more fragile and abstract but, at the same time, more liberating—people's faith in the U.S. government's ability and willingness to honor all dollars.

That faith would be a crucial step toward unlocking the dollar's full potential to mobilize the global economy at the end of the twentieth century. No longer constrained by a finite supply of bullion, the United States could now print more dollars than ever before, and it could borrow more money through the Treasury bond market than ever before.

At the time of the decision, however, the dollar's popularity was about to approach an all-time low. Politicians on both sides of the aisle were quick to criticize

Nixon's move as reckless. California Republican Bill Dannemeyer went so far as to maintain that leaving the gold system was an affront to God Himself. The U.S. congressman offered little elaboration on his claim, but he could have pointed to the foreign exchange market for obvious signs of the Lord's wrath. Over the next decade, the dollar plunged against many of the major European currencies and the Japanese yen. Currency traders at the time said dollar rallies were so few and far between that they were hard to recall. "The one thing you knew about the market was to bet against the dollar," says Bob Mammolito, who worked on the foreign exchange desk at Bank of America in New York at the time and now works for Taylor at FX Concepts. "Every day it went down, down, down. The only question was how much."

What caused the dollar to tumble so far? No longer set at a fixed rate to gold and other currencies, the dollar's value was now to be determined by the foreign exchange market. The first wave of currency traders, people like John Taylor at FX Concepts, appeared and would compare the state of the U.S. economy with that of its trading partners. They would then decide whether to buy or sell dollars based on their view of whether the dollar needed to strengthen or weaken. These traders looked at economic policy: Was a country being fiscally responsible or spending beyond its means? They examined whether a country was running budget and trade deficits, which were usually seen as bad for a currency, or running surpluses, which traders usually saw as a sign to bid up the price of a currency. Were a country's interest rates higher than other countries' and thus attracting foreigner investors to the currency? With the United States

stretched by military commitments abroad and new social programs at home, the dollar's position looked pre-
carious by most of these economic measures. Perhaps
most dire of all was the threat of inflation, which by
1970 was already running above 5 percent.

And yet the state of the American economy was
about to get much worse. In 1973 (a few months after
Nixon scrapped the final trading restrictions and allowed
the market to determine the dollar's value), one of the
plunging dollar's victims decided to fire back. The Organization of Petroleum Exporting Countries, or OPEC,
announced an oil boycott that would amount to a four-
fold rise in the price of crude oil, a move that rocked the
U.S. economy. The quadrupling in oil prices not only
forced Americans to wait for hours on line at the gas
pump, it sparked a vicious cycle that led to higher prices
on a wide variety of goods, from food to clothing, that
were affected by higher transportation costs.

Inflation was particularly detrimental to the dollar because it eroded the value of the currency, so that traders
would rather sell their dollars now than hold on to them
and watch their worth deteriorate further. A big source
of support for the dollar—then as well as today—is the
sale of U.S. Treasury bonds to foreign countries. Widely
regarded as the world's safest investment because they are
guaranteed by the U.S. government, central banks stash
reserves in these securities and private investors hold
them as "risk-free" investments that are highly liquid, or
easy to buy or sell in large quantities. But foreign governments can be hesitant to invest in U.S. bonds if the rate of
inflation exceeds the interest rate paid by the bonds because inflation would erode all their profits. This was

often the case in the 1970s. At the end of the decade, for instance, U.S. Treasury debt would pay 11 percent in interest, but with inflation running at 13 percent, overseas buyers would be losing 2 percentage points on their investment. This would obviously discourage them from putting money in dollar assets, and their pullback would drive down the dollar's value further.

OPEC's oil embargo was power politics. The Middle Eastern oil producers announced they would cease shipping petroleum to countries that supported Israel in the Yom Kippur War against Egypt and Syria. Yet, according to Greider, the dollar's plunging value was also crucial to the group's decision: "The OPEC price escalation was a direct and logical response to Nixon's fateful decision. Oil traded worldwide in dollars and if the United States was going to permit a free fall in the dollar's value, that meant the oil-producing nations would receive less and less real value for the commodity." Noting that the dollar had already lost one-third of its value at the time of embargo, Greider continued, OPEC countries "were grabbing back what they had already lost—and tacking extra dollars on the price to protect themselves against future U.S. inflation."

It was as if the oil exporters had answered Treasury Secretary Connally's bravado with some tough talk of their own—the dollar might be your currency, but it's not our problem. Because barrels of crude oil are sold in dollars, OPEC feels a direct hit whenever the dollar weakens. The reason is that these countries can buy less with those dollars in other markets around the world. If a cartel member, for instance, wants to buy anything in marks, francs, or yen, it receives fewer of those currencies in exchange for its dollars. So OPEC countries remain ready to raise oil prices during periods of a weakening U.S. currency to compensate themselves for the dollar's reduced purchasing power. As a result, oil prices tend to rise when the dollar falls and often ease when the dollar's value is rising.

While most Arab nations ended the embargo in March 1974, the seeds of inflation had been planted. For much of the rest of the decade, inflation would grow, rising to 8.8 percent in 1973, and it soon reached 12 percent. Making matters worse, the U.S. economy also suffered a recession, something that wasn't supposed to happen during periods of high inflation. Unemployment jumped to 9 percent, and economic output fell to levels not seen since the Great Depression of the 1930s. This unwelcome, and seemingly contradictory, mixture of rising prices and falling economic output came to be known as stagflation.

The U.S. government's questionable currency management only steamrolled the dollar further. In June 1977, Treasury Secretary W. Michael Blumenthal took the unorthodox step of suggesting that the United States would welcome a weaker dollar at a time when the greenback was already reeling. It was a misguided effort to stimulate demand for American exports, but his comments sent the dollar tumbling nearly 20 percent over the next year. Relief finally came in November when Washington withdrew $2 billion worth of marks and yen from the International Monetary Fund, funds the U.S. government used to buy dollars in the foreign exchange market and thus support the currency. Yet not long after this rescue package, the dollar decline resumed.

The Federal Reserve didn't have much better luck braking the dollar's fall or squashing inflation. Central banks slowed inflation by raising interest rates. Higher rates dampened economic activity by making it more costly for consumers and businesses to borrow to fund new projects or purchases. The restrained demand, in turn, limited the ability of companies to charge more for their products. Put another way, higher rates mean there is less money in the financial system chasing around goods and services, and hence less pressure to raise prices. But during the era of stagflation, when both the price of goods was rising and economic growth was sputtering, the Fed was understandably concerned that a lengthy period of high interest rates would sap too much growth at a time when the economy was already suffering. Consequently, the Fed raised interest rates but then usually felt compelled to stop before inflation was squashed.

In retrospect, Fed officials acted a bit like a doctor who had prescribed an antibiotic to a sick patient but neglected to authorize a big enough dosage. As a result, the patient became temporarily better—only to become worse later on because the bacteria causing the infection had not been killed. So the U.S. economy's inflationary problem might go into remission when interest rates rose, but it was never fully expelled and would flare back to life.

Arthur Burns, who served as the Fed's chairman from 1970 to 1978, bore the brunt of the criticism. Detractors accused him of ignoring inflation and cutting interest rates largely to curry favor with President Nixon. Despite the Federal Reserve's political independence, few Fed chiefs escape such allegations of knuckling under to domestic politics at some point in their careers—even Alan Greenspan,

critics say, did so when he voiced approval of the Bush administration's tax cuts. But Burns was considered more
culpable than most, and his actions were considered more
damning for the long-term health of the economy. Nixon
believed that the Fed's interest rate increases in 1959 led to
a recession in 1960. Nixon, then the sitting vice president,
took some of the blame for the slowdown in growth, and
he complained bitterly for years afterward that the recession cost him the 1960 presidential election.

As president, Nixon vowed it would be different. He
made his request for an accomodative monetary policy
explicit to Burns. If Burns resisted, negative stories about
him were planted in the media, *New York Times* columnist William Safire, a White House aide at the time,
wrote. Soon, the Fed chairman would make sure that interest rates came down and stayed down until after
Nixon's reelection in 1972. The rate cuts that gave a
temporary boost to the economy came back to haunt
it—and to ensure the continued decline of the dollar—in
the form of higher inflation.

President Jimmy Carter's choice to run the Fed, G.
William Miller, was considered even more ineffectual.
Miller never gained the trust of the Wall Street currency
traders and other market players who could determine
the dollar's value. They viewed the former chief executive officer of Textron Inc. as too reticent about raising
rates amid runaway inflation for fear of aggravating the
weakened economy. Some critics believed that Miller's
corporate background made him too comfortable with a
weak dollar because he saw it as lending a helping hand to
U.S. exporters. But as the prices of food and other goods
spiraled ever higher, even Carter seemed to have his

doubts. The president moved Miller to the Treasury department in 1979, making Miller's one-year tenure as Fed chairman one of the briefest in the central bank's history.

In July 1979, a somber, defeated-looking President Carter gave his famous Malaise Speech. He talked about America's "crisis of confidence" that was accompanying the persistence of high inflation and unemployment, and he sketched out a plan to combat these ailments. Carter also ruefully underscored the sad state of the U.S. currency: "We remember when the phrase 'sound as a dollar' was an expression of absolute dependability," he told the nation during the televised address, "until ten years of inflation began to shrink our dollar and our savings."

The next morning, the dollar fell in trading once again. The currency commanded only 1.82 Deutsche marks—half the value it had versus the German currency in 1971. Against the yen, the greenback now stood at 217.35 yen, down 39 percent over eight years. Foreign confidence in the dollar had slipped so dramatically that for the first time in decades, the U.S. Treasury was forced to raise money by selling bonds to the Germans—in marks. These sales, known as "Carter bonds" after the beleaguered president who approved them, were meant to give the U.S. government the ability to support the dollar by selling marks.

The Carter bonds were also an implicit reassurance to foreigner creditors that the United States would not try to inflate its way out of debt. Under dire circumstances, the United States could always pay off its dollar obligations by simply printing more dollars—leading to greater inflation and making U.S. bonds worth less to foreign holders. By issuing this foreign-currency debt, the United States was announcing to foreign exchange traders that it had an incentive to keep the dollar strong, since the weaker the dollar, the more dollars it would take to pay back debt denominated in marks.

The sorry sight of the superpower having to raise money in a foreign currency carried great symbolic weight. Without the Bretton Woods agreement to secure the dollar's central role, there was no longer a compelling reason to believe the greenback had to be the world's primary currency—especially with America seemingly unable to control inflation or fix its broken economy. Charles Kindleberger, an eminent economics professor at the Massachusetts Institute of Technology and a best-selling financial historian, seemed to sum up the dour mood at the time when he declared in a 1975 article that "the dollar is finished as international money." The only question, Kindleberger added, was what would replace it.

As dark as it looked for the dollar, an end to the currency's woes was closer than anyone suspected. The solution would require painful adjustments, and many wondered if the cure would prove worse than the illness. But in the end, it would keep the dollar at the core of the world economy, setting the stage for the even greater U.S. and global growth in the 1990s. The solution arrived the month after Carter's Malaise Speech. His name was Paul Volcker.

        •   •   •

Even from a cursory glance, the new Federal Reserve chairman was clearly different from his predecessors. At six feet, seven inches tall, Volcker towered over most everyone he met, though he was prone to slouching, as if always worried about bumping his head on something. As the new head of the Federal Reserve, he was arguably the most powerful man in the world of finance and banking. Yet he was notoriously frugal, often preferring an inexpensive Chinese restaurant to one of the capital's fine dining spots. Even so, Volcker was eminently qualified for the job. A graduate of both Princeton and Harvard, he had served in Nixon's Treasury Department (where he was among those who advised the president to end the dollar's fixed link to gold). More recently, he had been president of the New York branch of the Federal Reserve. By the time he was appointed in August 1979, he was as familiar on Wall Street as he was on Capitol Hill.

It was soon apparent that Volcker was prepared to do what previous chairmen would not or could not do: aggressively raise interest rates until inflation was brought under control.* With a series of interest rate hikes that pushed levels toward 20 percent—far higher than any of his predecessors had dared—the new Fed chairman was aware of the punishing toll this move would take on the economy and on individual lives. Bank lending would dry up, and consumption would slow. Millions would lose their jobs. Yet Volcker believed that only when inflation was crushed once and for all could the dollar and the broader American economy fully recover.

---

*Under Paul Volcker the Fed changed its operating process so that the central bank did not directly adjust the level of interest rates. Instead, the Fed would loosen or tighten the money supply, which in turn would cause commercial banks to react by raising or lowering interest rates. The Fed adopted this approach to provide it with some political cover, since this move distanced the Fed from making the unpopular choice of raising rates and causing economic pain. But the effect was essentially the same. If the Fed wanted lower rates, it would increase the money supply and the nation's banks would then lower interest rates in response. If the Fed wanted to push rates higher, Volcker would tighten the money supply, in effect forcing banks to raise lending rates.

Unsurprisingly, this was not a popular choice. While the bond market and banking community cried out for a Fed chairman who would slay the inflation demon once and for all, raising rates to unthinkable levels brought real suffering. Across the country, auto assembly plants, oil refineries, construction and property companies, and mom and pop shops would close down. Volcker's iron-fist monetary policy unleashed a recession that in many ways was harder on more people than any period since the Great Depression. Unemployment in 1982 surged above 10 percent (its highest level since 1940), with 12 million Americans out of work, most of whom were unable to draw unemployment compensation. That same year, 66,000 companies filed for bankruptcy protection (the most since the height of the Depression), and between 1981 and 1983, the economy lost $570 billion in output, according to figures from the Urban Institute, a nonpartisan policy research organization.

With the recession weighing on President Ronald Reagan's once-buoyant approval rating, members of his administration began to grouse about the soft-spoken, gentle giant at the central bank responsible for the pain. James Baker, Reagan's chief of staff, complained about Volcker to others in the administration: "How can he keep this misery going on so long?" *The Washington Post* reported that Henry Reuss, a Wisconsin Democrat and head of the Committee on Banking, Currency, and Housing, maintained that even other Fed governors "were wondering out loud whether it really makes sense to throw men and women out of work, and business into bankruptcy, in order to 'rescue the dollar.' "

Still, the Fed chairman did not waver. Nor did he hide from his detractors or avert his eyes from those aggrieved. In 1982, Volcker accepted an invitation to speak at the National Association of Home Builders' annual meeting. There he faced a disagreeable audience whose business had been decimated as badly as any in America. He told them that everyone would like to see the recovery begin, but more important than the timing of the recovery was that economic growth be sustainable in the years ahead. Otherwise, he explained, "the pain we have suffered would have been for naught, and we would only be putting off until some later time an even more painful day of reckoning."

During his periodic reports to Congress, Volcker maintained an air of detachment despite the venom directed his way. He wore rumpled pinstriped suits and a bemused expression that was obscured by smoke from the cheap cigars he puffed regularly. While his successor as chairman, Alan Greenspan, was famous for evading congressmen's direct questions with obtuse or cryptic responses, Volcker adopted an almost opposite approach. He would shake his head and answer his congressional inquisitors with what some considered overly simplistic or condescending language. So frustrated had congressmen and senators become with Volcker that some went so far as to draft legislation that would force the Fed to bring down interest rates—a direct and desperate challenge to the central bank's independence.

But before they had a chance to introduce the legislation (which stood a slim chance of passing, since most in Congress didn't really want to take on the responsibility of setting interest rates), the Fed decided it had gone far enough. With the economy in a tailspin, inflation had been cut by more than two-thirds to a rate of 4 percent from a high of 13 percent. In July 1982, for the first time under Volcker's command, the Fed pushed short-term interest rates lower. In the months that followed, the bond market rallied and long-term rates fell. The Dow Jones Industrial Average also rallied (indeed, though few would have guessed it, the blue-chip index was beginning a historic eighteen-year surge, during which the Dow Industrials would rise nearly fifteen-fold from below 800 to a high of 11722.98 in January 2000).

The dollar, however, may have been the biggest winner of all. From the middle of 1980 to August 1981, the greenback soared nearly 35 percent against a trade-weighted basket of currencies and would continue to climb higher. As interest rates came down, the Fed's victory at long last over inflation reestablished its credibility with the financial markets and with currency traders. That meant even as the central bank trimmed interest rates, the dollar wouldn't necessarily fall alongside them. People stopped worrying as intently about the dollar's demise. Even Kindleberger at MIT would have to admit that he had written off the world's most important currency a bit prematurely. For a while longer, at least, the dollar would remain unrivaled.

Not everyone thanked Volcker. Astonishingly, his name today can draw blank stares from the new generation of traders on Wall Street. Greenspan was dubbed "Maestro" for his adept handling of interest rates during what was largely a boom period, and today he collects six-figure checks for speeches on global finance. Volcker, meantime, has rolled up his sleeves for the less glamorous work of looking at issues of corruption at the United

Nations and in countries that accept money from the World Bank. During a speech I saw Volcker give in 2007, when he discussed the economy at a New York journalism scholarship dinner, it was a little sad to see the slouching giant at the podium. A few months short of eighty years old, he stooped over a microphone that, set a foot too low for his tall frame, muffled his words as he tried to speak above the rising chatter of an audience that seemed to have little regard for what he had done.

Yet it was Volcker who did the heavy lifting, strangling inflation and paving the way for the long period of prosperity during the Maestro's reign. Many, however, remember Greenspan's predecessor more for the pain he caused. During an interview at his Manhattan office last fall, where he works as a consultant, Volcker told me that he still gets stopped on the street and cursed by people who say he prevented their father from getting a home mortgage. Maybe the most bitter response of all came from the late Henry Gonzalez, a nineteen-term congressman from Texas. Volcker said he and Gonzalez were friends during the 1970s, when the future chairman was still in the Treasury Department. But during Volcker's time at the Fed, the Texas Democrat would go to the House floor almost every day to denounce Fed policy and call angrily for the chairman's impeachment. One day in the mid-1990s, long after he had left the Fed, Volcker found himself wandering around Capitol Hill. He had assumed that Gonzalez's regular tirades against him were mostly about politics, so Volcker thought he would visit his old Texan friend. He stopped by Gonzalez's House office, introduced himself to the receptionist, and requested to see her boss. She went off to relay the message.

A moment later, she returned to tell Volcker that the congressman refused to see him.

    •   •   •

By the mid-1980s, America's major allies began to have a new worry—that the dollar was getting too *strong*. Such a fear would have been unthinkable a few years earlier, when the greater concern was whether the dollar was about to lose its privileged position at the center of the global financial system. The suddenly powerful dollar was leading to inflationary pressure across the continent because the European currencies had become so weak versus the dollar, making the price of everything from Levi's jeans and Nike running shoes to a barrel of crude oil more expensive. In an effort to control that inflation, European central banks were forced to keep their own interest rates at relatively high levels, which in turn pushed their economies into an economic slowdown.

In West Germany, where finance officials were still haunted by the hyperinflation days of the Weimar Republic (at one point in 1923, $1 was worth one million marks), inflation remained society's biggest concern, and resentment toward the surging dollar grew. France's finance minister Jacques Delors referred to the dollar's surge as the equivalent of another "oil shock." In Britain, Prime Minister Margaret Thatcher complained to President Reagan about the seemingly unstoppable rise of the dollar. Despite her avowed devotion to free markets and disdain of government interference, Thatcher joined the chorus of European leaders demanding that Washington do something to halt the dollar's rise.

Not everyone in the U.S. capital was keen on the idea. For nearly a decade, the dollar had been derided as the monetary world's ninety-five-pound weakling. Many Treasury and Fed officials advised that a depreciation, if mishandled, could bring a return to such inglorious days. But political pressure was building—and not just from the Europeans. American exporters, especially automakers and other manufacturers, complained that the strong dollar made their goods less competitive abroad. Economists also warned that the U.S. deficit in the current account, a broad measure of all economic transitions and interest payments between a country and its trading partners, had ballooned to 3.5 percent of gross domestic product and could cause economic strains if it was not reduced. (Today, the current account deficit is about double that level and the warnings have become more dire. See Chapter 6.) With this in mind, Washington agreed to discuss group intervention to arrest the dollar's ascent.

So, on September 22, 1985, representatives of the so-called Group of Five (G5) leading industrial nations—the United States, Japan, West Germany, France, and the United Kingdom—met in New York City's Plaza Hotel and reached an agreement to devalue the dollar versus the yen and the mark. This arrangement, which became known as the Plaza Accord, called for several weeks of central bank intervention to weaken the dollar by 10 percent to 12 percent against the yen and the mark. These central banks spent around $10 billion to sell dollars and yen and marks.

The accord worked as planned. After the G5 ministers announced their intentions "for orderly appreciation of the main non-dollar currencies against the dollar," foreign exchange traders took the hint and decided to follow the path of least resistance by selling dollars, too. Within a week, the dollar had weakened by 12 percent versus the yen and 8 percent against the mark, and those declines continued over the next several months, well beyond what the G5 ministers had anticipated.

By 1987, the dollar had lost 38 percent of its value against the mark and 42 percent of its worth against the yen. The dollar's weakness caused new concern in Tokyo that the devaluation had gone too far and that Japanese exports would suffer. In Riyadh, the dollar's decline led to so much anxiety in the Saudi Arabian government, which was a big holder of Treasury bonds and other dollar assets, that Secretary of State James Baker had to offer reassurance that the dollar was not in crisis. Another accord was needed, the G5 Economies decided, this time to bolster the dollar. The ministers met this time in Paris, where the 1987 Louvre Accord orchestrated intervention to prop up the dollar's value again.

The dollar's value continued to fluctuate for several years, though one thing was clear: Reports of the dollar's demise had been greatly exaggerated. The 1970s runaway inflation and the Federal Reserve's loss of credibility with currency traders had led to sharp depreciations in the dollar's value. But in the end, the greenback's role as the primary currency for international trade and central bank reserves was never genuinely threatened. In fact, the lesson for a number of economists was that displacing the dollar from its throne would prove tougher than many had believed, even though the dissolution of the Bretton Woods agreement meant nations were no longer contractually bound to the currency.

At the end of the 1980s, the Berlin Wall came down and American capitalists could boast of an uncontested victory over the Soviet Union and, more broadly, over the socialist economic model. The sight of East Germans fleeing across the former border to marvel at the wealth, the variety of food and appliances—the sheer consumerism of the West—attested to the victory. Two years later, the Soviet Union itself would formally dissolve on Christmas Day. With its Communist foes vanquished, America could claim the spoils of winning the Cold War. Foremost, this meant nuclear disarmament and (the U.S. government hoped) a safer world. It also opened up dozens of potential new markets across the globe, not only in the former Soviet Union and Eastern bloc, but in their client nations of Africa and Asia. Former socialist governments, ex–party officials, and newly formed corporations would all look to participate in the free world's global economy, which had been effectively closed to them. To do so, they would seek the free world's currency of choice.

Under this new dollarized world, international trade and investment flourished as never before, unleashing a period of rapid growth rarely seen. In 1980, the world's total economic output stood at $10.9 trillion, exceeding the $10 trillion mark for the first time. Ten years later, the global gross domestic product had more than doubled to $21.7 trillion; by 2004, it had doubled again to $40.9 trillion.

Many factors—too many to list here—contributed to this burst in economic activity. Among the most important, trade barriers, such as tariffs that had slowed cross-border commerce during the first half of the century, gradually fell, thanks largely to multilateral negotiations under the General Agreement on Tariffs and Trade (which evolved into the World Trade Organization). The Internet and other telecommunications greatly enhanced the flow of information worldwide. That meant producers could get better information and could better target local tastes and product demands. Consumers, of course, could use the Internet to order goods faster and and at a lower price from around the globe. At the same time, financial markets became more sophisticated. Wall Street further developed futures and forward markets, derivative products that allowed companies to lock in a set price for commodities like steel or oil a year or more ahead of time. This enabled businesses to draw up plans for future investment, assured that even if commodity prices soared in the months ahead, they had protected themselves by locking in their costs with these financial instruments.

Yet none of these innovations would have mattered much if the world did not have a currency for conducting international business that would be accepted everywhere. As we've seen, the dollar was not the first currency to fill that role. The start of the twentieth century is often referred to as the first period of globalization: a time marked by the widespread acceptance of England's pound sterling, backed by the guarantee of gold, which gave people around the world the necessary confidence to transact with one another and be assured that their payments would be honored. This era of globalization, which teetered during World War I, eventually collapsed under the Great Depression.

The dollar assumed that international role after World War II. But it was not until the currency was freed from the gold standard that the global economy could shift into a higher gear. As international trade drove greater foreign demand for dollars, the United States could turn on the printing press, unrestrained by concerns that it should not print dollars worth more than it held in gold. This spike in the overseas demand for the world's currency means that 80 percent of the growth in the use of dollars since 1980 has been abroad. The United States, meanwhile, can borrow more money overseas through the sale of Treasury debt without fear, as there was in the 1960s, that foreigners could at any point demand gold in exchange.

Washington has come to rely on these foreign loans as a way to maintain—or increase—its spending while at the same time cutting taxes, counting on foreigners to make up the budgetary shortfall. American consumers, flush with cash from tax reductions and perennial borrowers in their own right, became especially voracious buyers of foreign goods. For much of the past decade, they seemed to almost single-handedly have kept the global economy afloat. Sluggish economies forced Europeans and Japanese to curtail their spending. The burgeoning markets of the developing world, meanwhile, spent years recuperating from the 1997 and 1998 financial crises and only recently began to pick up their consumption. But Americans rarely pulled back, even during soft spots in the business cycle. Economists cheerfully dubbed the avid U.S. shopper "the consumer of last resort"—suddenly as critical to the world economy's well-being as the central bank (in its role as lender of last resort) traditionally has been.

The world, therefore, owes a debt of gratitude to America's binge on foreign goods. But more recently, investors and governments have become worried that the by-products of America's debt-fueled consumption will be its undoing. American debt to foreign governments and its trade deficits have reached levels not seen before. Many economists, as we will see in the last two chapters, now worry that unless these debits are reined in, they will eventually erode confidence in the dollar— and could upend the world's economy with it. But first, a trip to Ecuador for an on-the-ground look at a phenomenon called dollarization. It illustrates how in today's economy, the dollar belongs to the world as much as it does to the United States.

CHAPTER 4

The Triumphs and Travails
of a Dollar Colony

E very evening around 6:00 P.M., the sun sets on
Quito, a vertiginous city that rises 9,300 feet
above sea level and is located a few miles south of the
equator. That's how regular the sun behaves near the
earth's beltline, and you can almost set your watch by
when it disappears behind the green hills of the Pichincha
volcano.

In human terms, the sun reveals a depressing sight.
Quito is the capital of Ecuador, a poor South American
nation of about 13 million people. More than half of
them—nearly 70 percent by one U.S. government
estimate—are mired in poverty. Violent crime is numb-
ingly commonplace in the capital, and guidebooks warn
against walking even two blocks in many districts at
night. The nation's rampant corruption vies each year for
the title of most extreme in the Americas. A high school
education is a rarity.

But it's in the political realm where Ecuador's shame
may be unparalleled. No less than eight presidents have
served over the past decade: three of whom are now in
exile, in prison, or both. One, dubbed "El Loco," was removed six months into the job for mental incompetence.

When I arrived in the capital in November of 2006, the day before the most recent presidential run-off, the entire city was festering under a temporary prohibition. My café's waiter explained, a bit sheepishly, that alcoholism is so rampant in Ecuador that every bar, restaurant, and shop is forbidden from selling liquor during the forty-eight hours before election polls close for fear people might otherwise be too blasted to show up.

And yet each morning, at 6:00 A.M., the sun rises on Quito. It is an awesome sight. The rays burst majestically through clouds nestled like great big swabs of cotton in the mountainside. The sunlight brightens the stately boulevards and palm-lined plazas of the well-preserved Spanish colonial section. It illuminates and flatters even Quito's shabbiest homes, perched perilously on the side of the lush hills in bright pastel blues, yellows, greens, and pinks. And as the sun rises, the city's inhabitants shout out defiantly that despite the crummy slums and the stickups and the broken political system—well, just look around outside! There is a new day dawning for Ecuador, they declare. And who's to say Ecuadorians are wrong? For, improbably, it is here that one of the great financial experiments of our time is unfolding.

Ecuador abandoned its currency, the sucre, in 2000 and adopted the dollar as its own. While few people outside of South America seemed to have been paying attention, this was a unique moment in monetary history. Throughout time, colonial outposts have been forced to use the currency of the mother country, from British pounds to Dutch gilder. The west African nation Liberia, founded by former black American slaves, had direct ties with the United States and pegged its first currency to the dollar in 1847. It then briefly used dollars in the mid-twentieth century before it resumed issuing its own currency. Today, dozens of countries use dollars for everyday transactions. China and other Asian countries have linked their currencies to the dollar, and up until a few years ago, Argentina pegged its peso at a one-to-one ratio with the buck. Panama even made the dollar an official currency, alongside the local balboa, more than a century ago when the United States began constructing the Panama Canal.

But Ecuador's decision is not quite like any other before it: The country chose to scrap—entirely and without any outside pressure—its own currency for the exclusive use of someone else's.

As bold a move as this was, some observers say Ecuador didn't have much of a choice. The economy was imploding. Two decades of poor policy decisions, natural disasters, a destabilizing border war in 1995 with Peru, and a long run of depressed prices for its major export commodities had left it in ruins. By 1999, inflation was surging, the sucre's value had deteriorated by 400 percent against the dollar, and the country was suffering a financial crisis that would ultimately wipe out many of its biggest banks. Ecuador's debt default had stymied the government's ability to borrow money in the international capital markets, and some Ecuadorian provinces were making noise about independence. "Dollarization was the result of a twenty-year crisis," Marco Naranjo Chiriboga, an Ecuadorian economist and former advisor to the central bank, told me in his Quito office. "There was no other way."

So with virtually no internal debate, and without the approval of Uncle Sam, Ecuador decided to embrace

what many Latin Americans have long viewed as the ultimate symbol of Yankee imperialism: the almighty buck.

Like a convalescing patient, Ecuador's economy got
worse before it could get better. During the traumatic
transition from sucres to dollars in 2000, inflation rose to
nearly 100 percent and unemployment spiked to as high
as 17 percent. Crime and misery were off the charts. An
estimated 1 million Ecuadorians—about one in every
thirteen—escaped between 1998 and 2001 to live abroad.
A year after dollarization, after forfeiting the right to
print its own currency and to run its own monetary policy, Ecuador had pitifully little to show for its radical
decision.

But then things began to brighten just a bit. Following a 7.3 percent economic contraction in 1999, Ecuador's economy expanded by a modest 2.3 percent in
2000 and by double that percentage the following year.
Even more encouraging, the scourge of inflation was
fading fast: It fell to 22 percent in 2001, to less than half
that in 2002, and to a meager 1.9 percent in 2004—one
of the lowest rates in the country's modern history. A
stable dollar enabled local companies to pursue normal
business plans again, confident that currency losses
would not overwhelm future profits. The dollar also
started to attract foreign investment back.

Today in Ecuador, banks are lending again. Corporations can borrow to grow their businesses, and families
can borrow to acquire more material wealth. The latest
Japanese- and European-made cars zip through Quito's
streets, and construction projects for new homeowners
dot the city's landscape. "The middle class is quite happy
now," Maria del Carmen Burneo, president of Seproyco,

a Quito-based economic consulting firm, told me in her office. "I didn't agree when they wanted to change the system. But for the past two to three years, things have been better."

Not surprisingly, the neighbors have noticed. About a year after Ecuador's move, El Salvador also elected to dollarize and Guatemala made it legal to have a dollar bank account and for companies to pay dollar salaries. Eduardo Lizano Fait, Costa Rica's central bank president, seemed to sum up the mood in Latin America at the time when he said in 2001, "It was a politically taboo subject four years ago, but nowadays everyone is talking about dollarization."

If people are still talking, however, they're doing so more quietly. No other Latin American country has taken serious steps toward dollarization since then. Some economists suggest Ecuador's success involved enough unique experiences—or, finally for this blighted country, some good luck—to question whether dollarization could be replicated elsewhere. Oil accounts for around half of Ecuador's export revenue, and the recent rise in petrol prices helped ensure that enough dollars flowed into Ecuador to make its dollar economy function. Billions of dollars in remittances from Ecuadorians abroad provided another outlet for the U.S. currency.

Other countries without those advantages might falter under dollarization. Moreover, Ecuador's poor people (which is to say, most of the country) do not have much to show from the economic turnaround; many complain they are worse off. Rafael Correa, Ecuador's leftwing president elected in the fall of 2006, has pledged to uphold dollarization for now. But he's no fan, blasting it in the press as a "perverse system" that he would like to replace with a South American regional currency as soon as possible.

Yet even as Ecuador's grand experiment continues to play out on the world stage, one thing is already clear: The globalization of the dollar offers poor countries a new option for running their economies. Call them dollar colonies. It's a choice that comes with many risks and tradeoffs and an obvious loss of financial independence. But the globalized nature of the U.S. currency has changed the rules of how the world economy functions.

In the early twentieth century, several Latin American and Eastern European countries struggled to accumulate enough bullion and get their fiscal houses in order so that they could adopt the gold standard. Most failed, leaving currencies backed by gold the exclusive hallmark of wealthy, mature economies. Those countries excluded from this affluent club were destined to suffer, to one degree or another, larger currency fluctuations and the economic dislocations that accompanied them.

Today, by contrast, even poor countries can make the world's most important currency their home currency, too. And they can enjoy at least some immediate benefits from that upgrade. They don't need to accumulate gold or silver or some other form of collateral. They don't have to meet financial targets set by the International Monetary Fund. They don't even need Washington's blessing. For as long as a great number of dollars circulate the planet freely and as long as a nation exports enough products priced in dollars or receives enough dollar remittances, the U.S. government would find it difficult to stop that nation's dollarization even if it wanted to. Nowadays, it seems, almost any country—even an economic and political mess like Ecuador—can be one bold decision away from joining the dollar colony. And if any doubt remained, Ecuador showed definitively that the dollar now belonged not just to the United States but to the world.

*   *   *

Ecuador's population today reflects the nation's roots: a blend of people of Spanish descent, indigenous Indians, and a small percentage of blacks. The predominant group, accounting for about two-thirds of the populace, are the mestizos, a mix of Indian and Spanish blood. Roughly the same size as the state of Colorado, Ecuador is bordered by Colombia on the north, by Peru on the east and south, and by the South Pacific Ocean on the west.

To understand how Ecuador's twenty-year crisis reached the boiling point in the final year of the twentieth century, it helps to know a little about the country's history. It's a legacy marked by a mistrustful and often bitter rivalry between the Sierra highlands, centered around Quito, and the steamy coastal region, anchored by Guayaquil, a tropical port town that today is Ecuador's business center and largest city.

The Sierra region was an important base for the Incan Empire. Traces of Incan culture, from dress to arts and crafts, can be found throughout Quito. And as the birthplace of Atahualpa, son of the Incan emperor Huayna Capac, the city figures prominently in the empire's history. But Ecuador's coast is separated from Quito by a rugged, nearly impassable mountain range that deterred foreign efforts to conquer it. By the time the Incas took control of Ecuador's coast, their empire was in tatters. They never had the chance to integrate Guayaquil, culturally or politically, into their society before the Spanish arrived in 1532. That cultural divide between the coastal and the mountain regions would deepen over the centuries, and it continues to shape Ecuador's government today.

During 300 years of Spanish rule, the areas surrounding Quito and Guayaquil developed separately. In 1822, Ecuador joined the South American independence movement of Simón Bolívar and became a part of the Republic of Gran Colombia. Eight years later, Ecuador broke off to form its own country. As the young nation developed, Quito became home to the more religious, landowning people, while the port town of Guayaquil was dominated by more commercial-oriented people.

Habitual tension between the two regions is responsible for Ecuador's fractious political development and greatly influenced its legal system. "Fearful that an administration largely from one region might impose its will on the other, the writers of Ecuador's constitutions tended to limit central political and administrative power, in particular, executive power," Paul Beckerman, an economic consultant, wrote in *Crisis and Dollarization in Ecuador*. The result was a weak central government—one that had little ability to push through politically unpopular measures and one marked by an intentionally weak president who could be removed by congress with relative ease (and, as it turned out, often for purely political reasons). This weakness is perhaps the main reason why Ecuador has suffered through so many presidents in so few years and why the central government could not act decisively during the years leading up to the 2000 dollarization.

In the early 1970s, the country enjoyed a tantalizingly brief period of prosperity. Led by a military government, Ecuador joined OPEC (it had left the organization in 1992 so it could increase oil exports but has recently rejoined) and its economy benefited greatly from the sudden surge in oil prices. Between 1970 and 1977, annual gross domestic product growth was an Asian tiger–like 9 percent. Ecuador's commercial banks took advantage of the good times by borrowing heavily from foreign banks. By 1976, however, inflation was rising, an El Niño storm had decimated much of the country's agriculture, and internal disputes within the government junta led to the restoration of a constitutional government and, in 1979, the election of Jaime Roldós Aguilera from Guayaquil as president.

Soon after, the government began a series of currency devaluations that would rock the economy and would lead inexorably to dollarization. As part of an International Monetary Fund program in 1982 to reduce the country's massive trade deficit, Ecuador agreed to devalue the sucre—which had been maintained at a rate of 25 sucres to $1 since 1970—by 25 percent. It devalued again the following year, and other minor devaluations would follow. But when U.S. banks became nervous and declined to roll over loans, Ecuador and much of Latin America suffered a debt crisis as the value of their currencies fell and the cost to pay back their dollar debt obligations rose. Ecuador's government in 1983 began to bail out the indebted banks by assuming their dollar loans, which transferred the debt problem from the private to the public sector.

The repeated currency devaluations also worried many in Ecuador's upper-middle class, who feared an erosion of their savings and began to park their wealth abroad in dollar accounts. By the 1990s, so much of the country's savings had migrated abroad that the government became concerned. Unable to restore enough confidence in the sucre to stem this flow, officials opted instead to ease restrictions on banks so that local institutions could also offer dollar accounts. This served as an incentive for people to keep their savings in the country.

In 1992, only 20 percent of all bank deposits in Ecuador were in dollars, and dollars accounted for less than 7 percent of the banks' loan portfolio, according to Beckerman. Those figures began to rise sharply in the late 1990s as the sucre weakened again and again. By 1999, more than half the bank deposits, and two-thirds of the bank loans, were in dollars. People started demanding that prices be set in dollars when selling homes or cars. Burger King restaurants abruptly shifted to charging dollars rather than sucre. The fast food chain, anticipating further currency declines, even set its own exchange rate for Whoppers.

Ecuador's worrying situation began to deteriorate into a full-blown crisis by the beginning of 1997. First, the presidential merry-go-round began to turn in comic-tragic fashion. Populist Abdalá Bucaram—the leader who referred to himself, usually in the third person, as "the crazy one"—was deposed by congress following a series of bizarre and sexually provocative antics. While in office, El Loco recorded an album of syrupy tropical songs he titled *The Madman Who Loves*. He mingled regularly with showgirls, boasted often of his love-making prowess, and on one occasion dined extravagantly at the presidential palace with Lorena Bobbitt, an Ecuadorian whose claim to fame was severing her philandering American husband's penis.

Accused of pilfering millions of dollars from the country and, according to some local accounts, much of the presidential silverware, El Loco—now the Madman Who Steals—fled in disgrace to Panama, where he was granted political asylum. His successor, the vice president Rosalía Arteaga, claimed the office as the next head of state. She served for only a few hours before the legislature decided instead to elevate its own leader, Fabián Alarcón, to the president's office.

At the same time, Ecuador began to suffer a number of setbacks not of its own making. Severe tropical storms in 1997 and 1998 ruined crops, forced big emergency spending (of money the government did not have), and reduced taxable income the state could ill afford to lose. These years were also marked by the currency and debt crises in Asia and Russia that punished Ecuador directly—such as the sudden collapse in Russian demand for Ecuadorian flowers—and indirectly. The widespread stock and bond market losses turned investors off to all emerging markets for years, and the fall in currency values across the developing world eroded Ecuador's cheap currency advantage in several export markets.

A terrible slump in the price of oil and other Ecuadorian commodities intensified the pain. When, in 1999, volcanoes at Guagua Pichincha and Tungurahua both erupted, destroying crops and further straining the country's

already overstrained budget, Ecuadorians began to wonder if even the gods had it in for them.

Whether any government policy at this stage could
have salvaged the economy is unknowable. But into this
toxic mix, Ecuadorian officials added some questionable
decisions. In 1998, to avoid instigating a politically
unpopular income tax, the government introduced a 1
percent tax on all financial transactions and bank withdrawals. The result was that many Ecuadorians began
storing their money outside of the banking system to
sidestep the new tax.

That was a blow to a banking system already teetering
on weak legs. Surging inflation made their loans unprof-
itable (the money the banks were paid back was worth
much less than the amount they loaned out) and it encouraged wealthier Ecuadorians to move more deposits
abroad. Authorities tried to limit the damage by fully
guaranteeing all bank deposits. When this, too, failed to
renew confidence in the system, the government took
the opposite tack: President Jamil Mahuad ordered, in
March 1999, a bank holiday—in effect, a freeze on all accounts to prevent any more money from leaving.

With people clamoring for their money back and
chaos looming if they were denied, Mahuad reluctantly
agreed to reopen some of the accounts. Between April
and December, about one-third of Ecuadorian checking
and savings deposits were withdrawn from the banks,
the equivalent of 3.1 percent of GDP. Things got worse
in September when the government defaulted on its foreign bonds. The default was particularly humiliating because it marked the first time any country had failed to
make a payment on so-called Brady bond debt (securities

that were backed in part by U.S. Treasury debt and named after the former Treasury secretary Nicholas F. Brady). They were created to help solve the Latin American debt crisis of the 1980s.

The sucre, which ended 1998 with an official value of about 7,000 sucres to $1 (though, of course, the black market rate for dollars commanded a much higher sucre price than that), had reached an exchange rate of 18,000 sucres to $1 by the end of 1999. It would reach a rate of nearly 30,000 sucres to $1 a few months later. As the Ecuadorian economist Naranjo pointed out to me, between 1979 and 1999, Ecuador's per-capita income had not grown at all. Astonishingly, the figures—a full two decades apart—were virtually the same.

If the 1980s were considered the "Lost Decade" for Latin America because the debt crisis had wiped out all growth, the 1990s were a much happier time. Most emerging markets sprang back to life and attracted waves of money from investors around the world. Despite the emerging market sell-off in stocks and bonds at the end of that decade, Mexico, much of Asia, and Eastern Europe had made real strides, growing and diversifying their economies as never before. During that 1979-to-1999 period, the global economy expanded by 89 percent, according to the International Monetary Fund. Many emerging markets grew much faster than that. Over the past fifteen years, China's economy has more than quadrupled in size.

But twenty years had passed for Ecuador, and what did this hungry, aching, self-divided country have to show for it? Not only were the economy and the standard of living essentially back where they started, nothing else seemed to have changed much, either. Ecuador was still captive to a weak central government and to a parade of ineffectual, sometimes clownish, presidents. The economy was still vulnerable to Mother Nature's wrath, and it was still a slave to the boom and bust cycles of its natural resources. Perhaps worst of all, Ecuador was still a victim of a currency destined to plunge in value because no one, least of all the locals, wanted any part of it. Just as the Ecuadorian sun would always set at the same time every day, the economy seemed stuck in an equally predictable pattern that would never change.

Not unless the people of Ecuador tried something radical.

•   •   •

On January 9, 2000, feeling boxed into a corner and desperate to do something, Mahuad took a radical step. He announced that he was submitting legislation to congress to dollarize the economy. With the stroke of a pen, he ended the sucre's 116-year existence and signed his country over as a dollar colony of the United States.

If no one in Ecuador could bear to think of themselves that way, the terms of the arrangement were nonetheless clear: In an effort to stabilize the economy, salvage an imploding banking system, and renew local and international confidence in a fragile financial state, Ecuador would effectively lose its monetary independence. It would sacrifice the right to print money and to devalue its currency to make its exporters more globally competitive. Ecuador's currency was now the dollar, and of course, only the United States could print that currency. That meant Ecuador would now have to rely on its companies to earn enough dollars on sales abroad. Otherwise the country would lack a sufficient amount of dollars to keep the dollarized economy running.

The move was a landmark act for Ecuador, but it was much more than that. It was fresh testimony to the unsurpassed global reach of the dollar—undeniable evidence that the dollar had become as much the world's currency as it was America's. Washington could try to stimulate or to restrict the dollar's use abroad, but it could not stop it. The dollar may be America's most potent symbol and precious export, but in January 2000, a tiny, troubled third world country reminded everyone that the dollar was in many ways now bigger than the United States. It belonged to the world economy.

Mahuad, however, wouldn't survive long enough to see his bold plan through. With frustration about the economy ready to boil over, and with the president facing widespread opposition to his controversial dollarization plan, Mahuad was overthrown in a revolt less than two weeks after his watershed announcement. An uprising, led by indigenous people and with assistance from military leaders, seized the parliament building, and the country was again briefly ruled by a military junta. As Alberto Acosta, Ecuador's energy minister and a prominent critic of the dollarization process, put it to me dryly, "The president said dollarization would be a great leap into the void. Two weeks later, he took a leap into the void himself."

Under pressure from the United States and lacking critical support from the masses, the military leaders gave way to Gustavo Noboa, Mahuad's vice president.

To the surprise of many, Noboa did not retreat from Mahuad's dollarization plan. In March, the new government led by Noboa ratified dollarization, and suddenly Ecuadorians were told they had six months to exchange their sucres for dollars. Any local currency held after that would be nothing more than a nostalgic souvenir.

Eventually, Ecuador would receive some outside help with this massive undertaking. Government officials had consulted briefly with Washington. The IMF, which had been critical of the Mahuad administration and its debt default, soon after dollarization resumed lending to Ecuador with a $304 million package. That in turn opened the doors for additional loans of about $1.7 billion from other foreign institutions, like the World Bank, providing a modest safety net as Ecuador walked its financial tightrope.

But, for the most part, dollarization was something that Ecuador did on its own. It was a move that even its proponents acknowledge was done in haste, with a sense of desperation, and without any established guidelines to help them. "There was no book to read on how to dollarize an economy," Eduardo Cabezas Molina, president of Ecuador's central bank and the country's former finance minister, explained to me in his Quito office, his eyes growing large as he recalled those days. "What we were attempting was unprecedented. We had no model to follow."

Dollarization's critics like Acosta make much the same point. "There was hardly any national debate or studies carried out," says Acosta, whose own study on alternatives to dollarization, such as controls on foreign capital, were widely ignored. Acosta recalls that a private economist from Venezuela came to Ecuador and convinced the government that dollarization was the only option. "Dollarization was presented as a solution to all our problems," he says. "The Venezuelan said the only thing dollarization couldn't cure was AIDS."

Yet, when the move finally came, there was a sense of inevitability about it. The government had no apparent plan for halting the sucre's fall, and the mood of the people was one of increasing anger and desperation. With U.S. trade accounting for about 60 percent of all trade in Ecuador, no other currency was seriously considered as an alternative to the dollar. Moreover, most of Ecuador's transactions at that point were already being carried out in dollars—about 90 percent, according to Naranjo. "With the sucre now depreciating significantly every day, the only alternative to dollarizing was clearly hyperinflation, which would have ended with dollarization in any case," Beckerman wrote of the historic decision. "In retrospect, Ecuador did not so much 'choose' dollarization as slide into it."

The government set the conversion rate at 25,000 sucres to $1, kick-starting a mad frenzy to unload the doomed currency. In the three months after dollarization became official, Ecuadorians exchanged about 95 percent of their sucre, or the equivalent of about $500 million worth of the local currency, into dollars, the Ecuadorian central bank says. American barges bearing trunks full of U.S. coins traveled south, while Ecuador's chartered flights from Miami touched down in Quito with more than $100 million in paper money from U.S. banks. The Treasury building in Quito became the scene of mass shredding rituals, as orange-tinted 50,000-sucre notes—worth $2 each—were permanently retired. By the end of April, less than two months after the government ordered dollarization, most of Ecuador's ATMs were dispensing only the U.S. currency. Grocery stores and other shops posted all prices in both dollars and sucres.

Still, the transition was far from smooth. The high conversion rate of 25,000 sucres to $1 made quick calculations a challenge for street vendors, taxi drivers, and shoeshine boys, many of whom would continue to insist on sucres. People were forced to wait on long lines, nervously trudging bundles or suitcases stocked with cash. Tens of thousands of teachers and hospital workers went on strike, joining mass demonstrations to call for higher wages and the end of dollarization. The strikes meant canceled classes for 3 million students. Only after police fired off tear gas were protesters prevented from storming the presidential palace.

The process got off to a rocky start in other ways, too. For one thing, dollarization was supposed to bring an end to the threat of hyperinflation; instead inflation accelerated. This was in part because shop owners and other merchants took advantage of the transition period to raise prices by rounding up on all small items. A piece of fruit that would have sold for the equivalent of 65 cents was marked up to $1, a taxi ride that was had for $2.35 would now cost an even $3.00 to cover the same distance, and so on until the price for most every good was several percentage points higher. These extra costs were, naturally, especially hard on the poor and retirees with minimal or fixed incomes. At the same time, government subsidies for gasoline, natural gas, water, and electricity were reduced to ensure that the government had enough dollars to make the system run. Inflation in 2000 rose more than 90 percent, a higher level than in the years leading up to the crisis.

The move to the dollar was also a blow to people's pride. "A national currency is like the flag," Cabezas of the central bank said, using a comparison that many Ecuadorians would make to me. "They are both symbols of the country." Not only had Ecuador ceased to fly its own banner, but taking its place on the flagpole was the Stars and Stripes—the symbol of the superpower to the north, giving people an uncomfortable feeling of being colonized by a foreign conqueror all over again.

Moreover, many people were slow to embrace dollarization because there was widespread belief it would be only a stopgap measure. Ecuadorians had been thrown from their economic ship and were drowning; the dollar was the country's life preserver. But surely, once help arrived through foreign loans or other assistance, the Ecuadorians would climb back on the deck, and the life preserver would no longer be needed. "People were convinced it was temporary," Pablo Buenaño told me one November afternoon, staring out of his office in the heart of Quito's business district. "Then we would go back to the sucre."

Buenaño is the deputy finance minister for the Andes Petroleum Company. Unlike most of the people I interviewed in Ecuador, Buenaño speaks fluent English. Since his company is now owned by China's Sinopec and his direct boss is Chinese, he's been working on that language, too. Dressed in a tailor-made shirt with a Mont Blanc pen poking out of his breast pocket, Buenaño has clearly done well under dollarization. But he says he speaks for most Ecuadorians when he suggests people see the dollar as here to stay. "Now that years have passed, people expect it to be permanent."

As the months rolled on, and Ecuadorians survived the rough transition to a dollarized economy, life returned to a semblance of normality. Inflation came down, banks resumed regular operations, and people went back to work. Despite early fears, use of the dollar did not equate to Quito taking marching orders from Washington. On the other hand, the U.S. currency did not turn Ecuadorian water into wine—or cure AIDS. Indeed, in many ways, Ecuadorian life was frustratingly similar to how it was before. Tropical storms still unleashed their merciless fury on the nation, ruining crops and threatening the country's economic welfare. Ecuador's political instability remained the butt of many jokes: In April 2005, congress removed yet another president, this time Lucio Gutiérrez, after street mobs screamed that he had abused power and demanded his resignation.

Yet, as Ecuadorians were starting to grasp, something real *had* changed. In the past, any of the country's natural or manmade disasters would have sent the sucre into a tailspin, aggravating an already bad situation by stoking inflation and intensifying the chances of a deeper crisis. Now, in the wake of Ecuador's latest political upheaval, the dollar played the opposite role: it brought a measure of stability. It was an anchor the economy could cling to to avoid drifting too far out to sea. After all, to the traders who fixed the dollar's value in the foreign exchange market, Ecuador was but a dot on a far horizon. The dollar was the global currency, its value determined by events in America and the other great economies of the world. The fickle whims of the Ecuadorian electorate would hold no sway on the dollar's worth.

The importance of this break from the past can hardly be overstated. The history of the third world's halting economic development has been one where plunging currencies and hyperinflation have been closely linked to broader financial crises, intensifying the misery and wiping out a population's life's savings. Now, Ecuador's currency—the same mighty dollar of the world's only superpower— would be a steadying influence during periods of volatility, rather than a malevolent force. "I can't imagine how bad it would have been during the political crisis without the dollar," del Carmen Burneo, the economic consultant in Quito, said, referring to President Gutiérrez's ouster. She shudders theatrically. "The currency would have collapsed. Again." Instead, the dollar's stability allowed many businesses to function even during that time of chaos.

•   •   •

The starting point for this restoration was the return to health of Ecuador's infirm banking system. With confidence in the currency restored, Ecuadorians gradually put their savings back into the banks. Falling inflation rates made loans a good business again. Many companies, now able to draft business plans without fear of further currency collapse, lined up to borrow once more. Not surprisingly then, probably no sector of the economy has thrived under dollarization as much as banking (at least the twenty or so that survived from around forty in the 1990s).

Guayaquil is the banking capital of Ecuador and, its proud residents here were quick to tell me, it has undergone a renaissance of its own. Considered one of the most dangerous cities in South America a few years ago, the local government has gone to great pains to beef up police presence and rebuild the downtown area in an effort to attract tourism. In contrast to mountainous Quito and its crisp evening weather, Guayaquil has a Caribbean feel to it. There's an unhurried pace at midday, and a thick stickiness in the air. Women negotiate the narrow streets with large trays of bright fruits on their heads, balancing bananas, green apples, and lush strawberries. Wet laundry hangs on rooftop clotheslines and traffic snarls through tight spaces without regard for painted lanes. The city's pride is the Malecon 2000, a sparkling riverfront promenade with blooming tropical gardens, ornate fountains, historical monuments, and a cool river breeze that offers a welcome respite from Guayaquil's oppressive humidity. Nearby are new cafés and food courts, four-star hotels, and two museums of local history and culture. The new airport is as clean, modern, and efficient as you'll find anywhere.

But for a first-time visitor, it is hard to imagine how awful the city must have looked a decade ago. For even after this expensive face-lift, Guayaquil is a dingy and depressing place. On the Avenida Panamá, where Ecuador's major banks have their headquarters buildings, armed guards, in groups of twos and threes, stand alert outside the entrances. Most are dressed in black, with Uzi machine guns slung tightly across their chests. When I stopped for a quick coffee around the corner from the Avenida, I was greeted at the door by a husky man with a wide smile and a pistol in his belt. He was the café's own armed security guard, installed there to put patrons' minds more at ease. Even in broad daylight, downtown Guayaquil has a sinister feel to it, and the city's less-menacing areas still look like the part of a town your parents always warned you to avoid.

Despite the city's threatening appearances, however, Ecuador's banks are mostly thriving. Their top executives are among dollarization's biggest cheerleaders. Guillermo Lasso Mendoza may be the most enthusiastic of all. As executive president of Banco de Guayaquil, he oversees operations of the country's second-largest bank with more than 120 branches nationwide. Sitting across from me in his board room this November afternoon, looking like the consummate banker in an immaculate gray suit with blue cuff links peeking through, he gets right to the point.

"Dollarization was a salvation for us," he says. He has the numbers to back it up. Banco de Guayaquil had $100 million in consumer loans on its books in 2000. By 2006, that figure had quintupled to $500 million. Corporate loans doubled over that period to $300 million. Meanwhile, bank deposits in 2006 stood at $1.2 billion, up from just $250 million in 2000. "All those increases are because of dollarization," he tells me. "People feel very confident because there's no problem with the currency and low interest rates. People can buy new homes and cars. Dollarization has improved the quality of life."

Importing the U.S. currency, however, is not the same as importing U.S. interest rates. Lasso says that car loans are now as low as 12 percent. But that's a far cry from the zero percent financing Detroit's big three automakers have offered. Mortgage loans, also starting at around 12 percent, are at least double what an American homebuyer with good credit could find at the time.

Moreover, a thirty-year mortgage doesn't exist; twelve years is more like it, and Ecuadorian motorists can expect no more than a five-year loan to buy a car.

Even so, these rates and loan maturities are a godsend compared with interest rates of more than 50 percent that Ecuadorian banks demanded in the late 1990s. And other borrowing rates look closer to what you'd find in the United States. Banco de Guayaquil's corporate rates can go as low as 6 percent to 7 percent, and credit cards may charge as little as 13 percent for cardholders who carry a balance. "That is probably less than the rate you pay in New York," Lasso brags to me.

If a rising standard of living isn't always easy to spot in Guayaquil, it's a little more obvious in some neighborhoods of the capital. "This is a poor country," del Carmen Burneo reminds me. "But look at the cars—they are all new. That's because of dollarization." Looking at the main roads, I see that she's right. There aren't so many high-end European luxury cars on the streets, but fewer clunkers than you'd expect, too. Even American automakers are picking up on this. General Motors said 2006 sales of cars and trucks in Ecuador had quadrupled to 87,000 since 2000.

At the Kia dealership around the corner from del Carmen Burneo's Quito home, the showroom is buzzing. It's stocked with minivans, sedans, and SUVs. It looks no different from thousands of auto dealerships in the United States. Susana Rivera, Kia's head of finance here, speaks in rapid Spanish as she relates her company's brisk business in Ecuador. Kia opened its first Ecuadorian outlet in 2000. It now has six showrooms and nationwide sells an average of 150 cars a month. The most popular model is the four-wheel-drive Sorento, which commands $34,000. The least-expensive model, the Picanto sedan, goes for $11,800. All you need is a loan and 15 percent cash down to drive one away. Ecuadorian salaries have stayed about the same over the past few years, Rivera says, but access to credit has greatly expanded. "In the past, there was no real middle class," she tells me. "Now you see one. It's helped that the banks stopped being afraid to give loans."

When the customers drive the new cars out of the dealership, many speed off to homes recently constructed. Quito's skyline doesn't yet resemble that of the Asian boom capitals of the 1990s, when the cityscape of places like Bangkok or Jakarta looked like erector sets. New homes are going up here at an impressive pace all the same. Two-story buildings are being razed so that six-story buildings can rise in their place. Just north of Quito, only a mile or so from the equator, suburbs are sprouting up like crabgrass. Many are still empty, and some are half-finished. But from the completed models, you could easily confuse this corner of Ecuador with the California suburbs.

The property rebound has been remarkable. With the exception of banks, no business may have suffered as much from Ecuador's financial crisis as real estate. "It was terrible," recalls Milton Validivieso, who runs Corporation Enrorno, a property management and construction company in Quito. He has been in the property business for close to a quarter century and has been witness to some tough times. Inflation for the industry, at about 120 percent, was twice the national average in 1999. The sucre's massive devaluation meant that the cost of raw materials like aluminum, copper, iron, stainless steel, and glass shot up. He had to buy a year's supply of materials ahead of time to hedge against inflation or currency depreciation. In the 1990s, he'd start projects only to abandon them midstream when buyers backed out or never materialized. By the time Ecuador had decided to dollarize, his firm had stopped building—or even planning any new units. "It was hard to have a fixed budget for more than six months," he shares with me. "You couldn't tell what would happen."

This afternoon, Validivieso is talking with enthusiasm about the industry's comeback. We hold our conversation in his office, which is on the ground floor of a new residential building he's constructing. His bright blue eyes flicker. Dressed in a navy blue sports coat with brass buttons and a soft blue shirt, he looks relatively affluent. This is one of three projects his firm has launched since he began taking on new work again in 2003. When completed, the building will hold sixteen units of one- and two-bedroom apartments; thirteen have already been sold for an average price of $90,000. Many of the new owners, Validivieso says, are buying homes for the first time.

As he tells it, many things are breaking right for the property business these days. The industry's inflation rate is down to 8 percent a year, and the only reason it's that high is because the price of iron is rising rapidly. All the banks are lending again, and consumer demand is healthy. Validivieso is not the unqualified booster for dollarization that Lasso is. He's worried that if oil prices dip again, Ecuador will struggle to find enough dollars to keep the system running. "We have had a lot of luck," he says. "We can only survive if dollars come in. But it is impossible to return to the sucre."

To my surprise, I found that even some businesspeople whose profits were badly jeopardized by dollarization were finding innovative ways to adapt, relying on an ingenuity that they had never before tapped.

Take, for instance, Hugo Torres. He's a hotelier and tour operator in the Mariscal area of Quito, home to the city's nightlife district. Charging clients from Europe and North America in dollars while paying his local staff and suppliers in sucres, his business was geared to exploit Ecuador's currency devaluations. The more the sucre fell, the fewer dollars he needed to make all his payments. So the country's switch to the U.S. currency was a financial catastrophe for his business. Foreign tourists who suddenly found Quito too expensive took their travel budgets elsewhere, to cheaper places like Peru or Nepal. At the same time, his bills—telephone, electricity, grocery—were skyrocketing now that they were all in dollars. He estimates that his cost per employee per month has jumped to $250 today from $70 before dollarization.

To counter this—to survive, really—he was compelled to change his business strategy. He turned his focus upscale and appealed to a wealthier clientele. With his savings, he replaced his aging fleet of boats with new luxury boats for tours of the Galápagos Islands. Tourists now ride in style on ninety-foot-long Motor Catamaran yachts with three decks and sleeping quarters for eighteen passengers. He raised the admission cost to $250 a day from $120. To his stable of $16-a-night Quito youth hostels, he's adding a boutique hotel where plush satellite- and Wi-Fi–equipped rooms will go for $120 to $160 an evening. And he's become a more aggressive marketer, regularly attending travel shows in the

United States and Europe to drum up business and make new contacts.

While his business is healthy now, his profits since dollarization still trail those during the heady days of massive devaluations. "We have to sell a lot more to the same number of tourists," Torres says somewhat despondently, shifting uncomfortably in his office chair inside one of the hotels. He pauses for a moment, as if to consider carefully what to say next. Then he resumes. "Now we have first-class hotels. In the long run, I think it's a better thing."

Across town, in a peach-colored Spanish villa, the Arbusta floral company looks even more prosperous. Bundles of fresh red roses adorn every table, and the air is fragrant with their scent. Floral exports were supposed to be one of the biggest casualties of dollarization. In the beginning at least, it was tough on all of them. Foreign buyers attracted to the cheap price for Ecuadorian flowers when the sucre was in a tailspin balked at the inflated prices under dollarization. Many customers turned instead to Colombian sellers with their cheaper peso prices. A year into the currency switch, about 10 percent to 15 percent of Ecuador's floral companies had posted out-of-business signs.

"There's no question that we benefited from endemic devaluation," says Miguel Mascaro, a cofounder of Arbusta. "Then in 2000, we had the inverse. Hyperinflation in dollars." Mascaro ticks off for me a laundry list of rising costs when the country switched currencies: staff salaries, fertilizer, payments to truck drivers, and so on. Moreover, since two-thirds of his sales come from clients in the United States, the new price tag on his flowers in dollars suddenly looked excessive.

So like Torres's strategy for the tourism business, Arbusta shifted gears and took aim at the top-end of the market. Mascaro, who has a master's degree in business administration from Cornell University, invested in new filters and compounds to breed roses that were bigger, brighter, and longer-lived than any Ecuador had previously produced. He installed special containers for growing more homogenous, superior carnations. And he sought out premium wholesalers in the United States who were willing to pay top dollar for a best-of-breed product.

The moves have paid off handsomely: Mascaro says profits are up nearly 50 percent from pre-dollarization levels, boosted by profit margins that have expanded to 25 percent from 10 percent. While he had to retrain his employees to work with the new technologies, most have stayed on. Indeed, Arbusta now employs 750 people, a 50 percent increase from staff size in the late 1990s. He counts some of these employees among Quito's embryonic middle class, pointing to the new cars parked outside his office and to the DVD players, stereos, new refrigerators, and other appliances they stock their homes with. "When we had sucres, it was impossible for most white-collar people to enjoy these things," he says.

Torres's and Mascaro's ability to adapt to a tougher competitive environment is still rare in Ecuador. This sort of transformation requires a good deal of capital to invest in new technologies or products and the good business sense to know how to do it. Many other firms in their industries, which relied primarily on their product's comparatively cheap prices, are struggling to survive. Yet, when I mention this to Raul Daza Martinez, dean of the economics faculty at Quito's Catholic University, he argues that the private sector is learning to become more competitive. Today, Ecuador exports more than 1,000 different products, he tells me, from textiles to wooden furniture to glass containers. During the sucre days, the country relied primarily on selling basic commodities abroad. "The dollar challenge has led to greater diversification among exporters," he says.

Not only that, he continues, but tax collection is easier. Previously, companies regularly reported losses that they blamed on currency devaluations. Now the accounting system is all in dollars, and thus more straightforward. The result is higher tax revenue that is being used, slowly but increasingly, for the benefit of the broader society, not just the upper crust. Government's expenditures on education and health care, Daza notes as an example, have increased to 5 percent of Ecuador's GDP from 2.7 percent a few years ago. He adds that other economic indicators are positive, too: Individual consumption is up among all segments of the population, unemployment is down, and poverty, especially urban poverty, is falling.

Just maybe, after twenty years of frustration and false starts and negative progress, a new day is dawning for Ecuador after all.

* * *

Alberto Acosta surely doesn't see it that way. An economics professor trained at Germany's University of

Cologne, he is renowned for his left-wing beliefs and af-
filiations. It would not be a stretch to say he considers
dollarization a fraud perpetrated on a desperate people.
"Ecuador under dollarization has been an example of
what you shouldn't do," he says. The day I see him,
Acosta is still basking in a political victory. His close
friend, Rafael Correa, was elected president two days before. Acosta would rise to new heights of power himself,
being named as this oil-rich country's new energy minister only a few hours after our meeting.

It is in Correa's Quito office where I met Acosta. A
campaign poster declaring "La Patria Vuelve!" (The
Homeland Returns!) is unfurled above the office receptionist's head. Despite his populist views, Acosta is clearly
a discerning man of fine tastes. He's wearing a beige cash-
mere sweater, crisp blue jeans, and designer tortoise-shell
eyeglasses. His oval face is deeply tanned. He's trim, with
wavy black hair gently speckled with gray. If you didn't
know Acosta's background was academia, it wouldn't be
hard to guess. He has a habit of speaking like a lecturer
addressing a classroom and dispensing pearls of wisdom.
"When dollarization happened there was no space for discussion," he begins. "There was a general stupefaction of
the people." As Acosta sees it, people have mistakenly attributed Ecuador's newfound stability to dollarization,
when the rightful recipient should be the powerful recent
spike in oil prices. "The apparent benefits of dollarization
have been a mirage," he says, and then he dissects them
one by one.

It's true that inflation has come down, he notes, but
it took five years to return to internationally accepted
levels. Interest rates also have come down, but they have

recently ticked up again and are higher than those in neighboring countries like Peru, Costa Rica, and Chile. This, he points out quite rightly, is because the central bank under dollarization has, in effect, lost its ability to set interest rates. Instead, that job has been taken over by a handful of the largest commercial banks, which get a better payoff on their loans if rates remain at current levels.

Acosta also charges that economic growth has been subdued under dollarization, with many exporters, from car part makers to refrigerator manufacturers, suffering. To see what might one day happen, he points to Argentina. That country's currency system, which pegged the dollar at a one-to-one ratio with the local peso, was also adopted during a crisis period to slay inflation. It worked throughout the 1990s until a series of currency devaluations in Brazil and other Latin American export rivals caused Argentine companies to lose their global competitiveness. Sales abroad plummeted. Argentina was soon mired in recession and, because of its strict currency peg, had its hands tied in terms of monetary policy. Running low on dollars, Argentina defaulted on a record $140 billion in foreign currency debt. With the population on the verge of revolt, the government felt compelled to devalue in 2002. While Argentina's and Ecuador's currency systems and economies are not the same, there are enough similarities to raise concern.

Like most dollarization critics, Acosta raises the possibility that even the successes are the product of fortunate circumstances—that only the oil price spike and the $2 billion in annual remittances from overseas Ecuadorians allowed the system to function by flooding the country with dollars. Should either tap be turned off, or even tightened, Ecuador could face another crisis, Acosta asserts.

At this point, Acosta politely excused himself to go to a meeting. But he could have continued with other compromises that dollarization has forced on Ecuador. The profits a government makes from printing currency, known as seigniorage (essentially the difference between the face value of money and what it costs to print it), cease to exist for a country that no longer prints a currency. The Ecuadorian central bank estimates this amounts to a $20 million annual loss of revenue for the government.

Ecuador's central bank has also lost its status as a lender of last resort to the banking system, since it cannot print currency to bail out troubled banks. Instead, the government has set aside an emergency fund in dollars, and each private bank is required to contribute 1 percent of its deposits to the fund. But in the event that this fund is ever depleted, the central bank could do little else to help the banking system. Nor has dollarization managed to lift Ecuador's government credit rating. It is still a low-grade "junk" credit, which means that the country's ability to borrow in the international markets remains very limited and punitively costly.

Dollarization has unleashed other unwelcome effects that few anticipated. The prospect of dollar wages has attracted laborers from Peru and Colombia seeking work in Ecuador. Many of these transplants are illegal and take away potential jobs from locals. Even the legal workers from abroad tend to remit much of their wages back to their home countries, withdrawing money from Ecuador's local economy. Del Carmen Burneo says that the new consumption habits have their dark side, too. For instance, all those new cars on the road have made Quito's pollution problem much worse. On particularly bad days, walking in the city's valley can feel like entering an airport smoking lounge. She also worries that unless the country's working class gets better access to bank credit, the already yawning income disparity in Ecuador could get much worse. "The middle class are certainly better off," she says, "but the poor are stagnating."

·   ·   ·

The town of Calacalí is a few miles north of Quito. It's reached by a winding mountainous road that's notorious for traffic accidents and, like much in Ecuador, is to be avoided at night. On the way from the capital, you pass by beautiful Pululahua, a volcano that last erupted about 2,500 years ago. It is now home to a verdant hamlet that sprung up inside the crater of the extinct volcano. Bird watchers from across the globe drive by Calacalí on their way to view rare species in nearby towns. But Calacalí itself doesn't offer much to see: a public square, a main road, a handful of small shops, and cramped restaurants. It's not the poorest village in Ecuador, but it's the sort of place where people are in danger of stagnating.

Calacalí residents, for the most part, don't see how dollarization has changed anything for them. "It doesn't make any difference to the poor. We don't get any richer," says Seugundo Gallardo, whom I met as he shuffled slowly toward the main square. Gallardo gives his age as seventy-eight. His scruffy white beard looks about four days old, and the brim of his tan hat is stained dark with sweat. A former gardener, he says he's retired now and receives a $200-a-month government pension. Like others on a fixed income, he complains that the dollar's introduction led to a drastic markup in prices (as shops rounded up to the nearest dollar) and that he feels he can buy less today than he could five years ago. "All the money I have goes toward food," he says.

Maria Tandalia has much the same complaints. A thirty-four-year-old mother and housewife with a braided ponytail that falls halfway down her back, she says her life is harder since dollarization. Nothing, she says, is cheap anymore, not even the smallest goods or food. "Everything costs at least 50 cents now," she says. "Most things are a dollar." Even though most anyone can open a bank account in Ecuador with as little as $200, many poor Ecuadorians still don't trust banks, and some have to save for a while to reach $200. Tandalia says her family has no savings account. Even if she did, she would be unlikely to qualify for a loan. People like her felt more equal before the dollar came. "We want the sucre back," she sums up.

Back in Quito, the people who are building new homes for middle-class and wealthy Ecuadorians don't sound much more satisfied. Just behind the office where Validivieso's new apartment complex is being erected, construction workers are busy laying brick and pounding in nails. When the day is over, many of them will take a bus as far as it goes up the mountain. Then they'll walk another half-mile, or more, up the steep hill. Buses don't go as far as the top, where the poorest people live.

Taking a break is Bolivar Carrillo, a gardener working

on the landscaping of the construction site. He's leaning casually on the handle of a large shovel stuck in the ground as he talks to me. From his dark, lined face and straight, jet-black hair, I'd guess he's close to pure indigenous descent. He says that he supports a family of a wife and three kids on a salary of $50 a week. "My salary is the same but prices are higher since the dollar," he says. But given the chaos, and the spike in prices that surrounded the currency change seven years ago, he shakes his head to indicate he wouldn't welcome a return to the sucre. "I've gotten used to the dollar."

Even in Calacalí, there are signs that not all is stagnation. At one corner of the main square, Jenny Morales welcomes customers to her grocery store. She is a middle-aged woman, squat, with long black hair and a ballpoint pen tucked behind her ear. The cramped shop is about the size of a college dorm room, and everyone who enters greets Morales with a wave and a cheerful "*Buenos días.*" Some customers pause in front of the TV, which is showing a Mexican soap opera. Her store stocks a number of things you wouldn't find in an American grocery store, like chicken heads and feet that customers will use to make soup. But other shelves are filled with a variety of foreign products, from Coke and Sprite to Frito-Lay chips and Bacardi rum. Morales says that she got the money to open the store from a bank loan in 2002 and that three years later, she had paid it off. The store is all hers now, she says proudly, adding, "Yes, the dollar made that possible." But her store is busy, so she excuses herself to go help a customer.

•   •   •

On New Year's Day 2001, El Salvador discarded its own currency and signed on for the dollar. For Ecuadorians who experienced the wrenching transition to the U.S. currency, some of the bewildering scenes in El Salvador during those first few months would have been achingly familiar: widespread confusion over calculating exchange rates, the initial refusal of some vendors to accept dollars, and the "rounding up" of prices that boosted inflation.

But in most other ways, the two situations could hardly have been more different. El Salvador was suffering no financial crisis at the time of its dollarization. It wasn't even experiencing any notable currency depreciation (the conversion rate, for instance, was 8.75 colónes to $1, as opposed to Ecuador's 25,000 sucres to $1). Rather, the Central American country saw dollarization as the next logical step toward faster growth by reducing foreign exchange risk, creating conditions for interest rates to fall, and attracting more foreign investment.

Since 1992, the last year of a civil war that claimed 75,000 Salvadorian lives, the country's 7 million people have seen their economy grow at a steady clip. During that period, El Salvador was able to cut its poverty rate of 66 percent nearly in half. And perhaps more than any other Latin American nation, El Salvador followed America's free market prescription for economic growth. That included privatizing banks, utilities, and the public pension system. The government also reduced import duties and improved enforcement of intellectual property rights. In all likelihood, officials would have gone ahead with dollarization whether Ecuador had gone there first or not. El Salvador's economy continues to expand and the poverty level continues to fall, though it is hard to separate the effects of dollarization from those of other economic reforms.

Shortly after El Salvador joined Ecuador and Panama as the third Latin American country with a dollarized economy, Mexican finance minister Francisco Gil Díaz confidently said that if dollarization works in Ecuador and El Salvador, "others will follow." That no other country has done so doesn't mean that dollarization isn't working. But it does suggest that most Latin American countries are neither as desperate as Ecuador was in 2000 nor as enthusiastically free market oriented as El Salvador was in 2001. For a combination of political, economic, and nationalistic reasons, most countries seem to prefer to stick with their own currencies.

Cabezas, for one, says he won't evangelize about the dollar to anyone. "Ecuador does not export dollarization," the central bank president asserted, wagging his left index finger at me. "It is a unique experience. We don't recommend it for other countries." Why? He cites the same two crucial factors that most observers say have been key to Ecuador's functioning dollar economy: the high oil price and remittances from a million expats. (Some people also confided that sales of illegal drugs, which are exported and sold for U.S. currency, represent the third leg of the stool that supports Ecuador's dollarization, though naturally tracking those numbers is difficult.) Without these bountiful remittances and reliable dollar sales from a highly prized export, dollarization would be hard pressed to work anywhere.

Washington hasn't taken an active approach in promoting the dollar as a substitute currency, either. American Treasury officials have met intermittently with their Ecuadorian counterparts since the switch to dollars, including a 2003 meeting in Washington between Treasury secretary John Snow and a delegation from Ecuador of government and bank officials. But a Treasury spokeswoman declined to comment on the details or substance of meetings with individual countries. Congress has barely addressed the issue. The Senate held hearings on dollarization in 1999 and again in February 2000, shortly after Ecuador announced its plan to dollarize. Later that year, the Senate Banking Committee passed the International Monetary Stability Act, which proposed that the United States share some of its seigniorage earnings with countries that adopt the dollar as a way to encourage the currency's use abroad. The effort was led by Senator Connie Mack of Florida, the chamber's resident champion of dollarization, who argued that it would increase U.S. trade and lower America's transaction costs. But the bill never made it as far as a full Senate vote.

At the same time, currencies in Chile, Bolivia, and other Latin countries have become more stable in recent years. That would make a potentially traumatic and politically humbling conversion to the dollar less appealing, Professor Daza at Catholic University points out. For Colombia and Peru, much of their economic activity is already conducted in dollars: 80 percent of the total worth of economic transactions in those countries is dollar-based, Ecuador's central bank estimates. In Peru, more than half of commercial bank deposits are in dollars, and the U.S. currency is routinely required for many purchases, such as for airline tickets, and for many services, such as for cable television. Large grocers will gladly accept dollars, too, and many offer prices only in dollars.

But the new administration under President Alan García—who was elected in 2006 for his second stint as president sixteen years after the first one ended—has been implementing policies to nudge Peru away from dollarization. The government has passed a law that requires shops to price all goods in the local currency, soles, in addition to dollars. Even before that, there were signs that Peru's dependence on dollars was gradually ebbing. Government figures, for instance, showed that by mid-2006, dollar loans represented about two-thirds of all loans made by Peruvian banks. As high as that figure sounds, it was down 15 percent from 1999. "De-dollarization has been a very slow process, but we're on the right track," Peru's central bank president Oscar Dancourt told Reuters. He predicted that the country will cut its dollar usage by half within a decade.

In Ecuador, President Correa has never hid his disdain for dollarization. On the 2006 campaign trail, he told reporters that "dollarization is bankrupting us. It is part of the problem and not the solution," according to the Dow Jones Newswires. The president didn't call for a return to the sucre, but bristling at the thought of being a dollar colony, he has repeatedly suggested that an Andean or a South American currency is a goal of his administration.

But how realistic a goal? The European Monetary Union was decades in the making. Even then, the infant euro had to rely on the hard-won credibility of the Deutsche mark and German central bank. There is no German equivalent in Latin America: No country has a long enough track record of monetary stability to serve as a foundation for a regional currency.

Besides, Ecuadorian officials may face as much opposition to leave the dollar as they did when they embraced it. Polls show about 70 percent of Ecuadorians support keeping the dollar. Even Correa had to clarify for a worried electorate that he had no immediate plans to end dollarization. "Ask the gardener or bricklayer if he wants to switch from a dollar to a bill called Hugo Chávez," Lasso instructed me, referring to Venezuela's leftist president. "Obviously they will say no."

Despite signs of a growing middle class and a higher standard of living for some, Ecuador's economy still has numerous problems. Economists say that public spending on infrastructure—things like public transportation, health care, and education—is insufficient to improve most of the country's quality of life. The mean streets of Guayaquil are testimony that Ecuador's mending cities are still a long way from being prosperous, or even particularly safe. Politically, the nation remains divided along geographical lines.

Ominously, foreigners also remain skittish about making long-term commitments to Ecuador, in part because of the country's spotty record for honoring contracts. These concerns have only intensified since President Correa's election in November 2006. Correa and other members of his administration have said that they consider much of Ecuador's foreign debt—money borrowed by previous regimes—as "illegitimate." Some of these officials have even hinted darkly that the government might delay or renegotiate these debt payments. Economists also worry that the budget plans Correa outlined for the fiscal year 2008, which call for large increases in government spending, could strain the country's finances and leave few contingency funds available to stabilize the economy in the event of a crisis. "A fiscal expansion growing out of control would make dollarisation [sic] unsustainable," according to Global Insight, a Waltham, Massachusetts, economic forecasting and consulting company.

Merely adopting the dollar isn't a substitute for resolving such issues of mismanagement and mistrust. Some observers think that if these dilemmas aren't addressed, problems will fester and could eventually threaten Ecuador's ability to sustain dollarization, as it did with Argentina's currency peg. Charles Calomiris, a professor at Columbia University's business school who has served as a financial advisor to the governments of Mexico, El Salvador, and Argentina says, "I don't see any evidence that Ecuador has the political and financial structures to prevent an eventual crisis. When that crisis happens, you'll see them end dollarization so that they can turn on the money printing press again. That's what always happens."

Professor Daza takes a different view. He doesn't see dollarization as a panacea. Rather, he considers it a uniquely stabilizing force that has created the foundation for Ecuador to build a more productive economy—if the government has the will to act on the more pressing issues. "We've thrown our lot in with the dollar," he surmises. It may take years before we can say who is right. But whatever comes next, dollarization is a policy choice that poor countries like Ecuador wouldn't have had a few decades ago. It remains to be seen whether that privilege will amount to anything.

CHAPTER 5

The Dollar's Buyers of Last Resort

The countries that hold U.S. currency and securities in their banks also hold U.S. prosperity in their hands. That prospect should make Americans uncomfortable.
—LAWRENCE SUMMERS,
former U.S. Treasury secretary

Few countries have as complicated or as intense a relationship with the United States as does South Korea. It is often a love-hate relationship, to be sure. But that description applies to many countries these days. South Korea's case is special. The peninsula nation hosts 27,000 American troops amassed to protect a country that has been at war, if not in open conflict, with its neighbor to the north for more than fifty years. It is the largest U.S. military presence in the Pacific, and even the nation's capital, Seoul, has made visible concessions to the U.S. army. Nestled near the city's center, where you might expect to find a temple or a park or a piazza with a bubbling water fountain, lies a 635-acre U.S. military base. It is rimmed by a ten-foot-high wall and topped with menacing-looking barbed wire to keep out the enemy—and curious locals, too.*

The base is a daily reminder that this prosperous and economically self-reliant nation still counts on its big American brother for national security. In more ways than one, South Korea owes its very existence to the United States. General Douglas MacArthur's troops drove out the invading North Korean army in 1950, and many security experts believe that only the formidable presence of the American military deters the North Koreans from attacking again. Like any proud people, South Koreans view a massive foreign troop presence with marked ambivalence. Having hosted the 1988 Olympics and the 2002 soccer World Cup and being home to companies like Samsung Electronics and Hyundai Motors, South Koreans are prouder than most. They may fear what would happen if the American troops were to leave their country, but having pulled themselves up by their own economic bootstraps, South Koreans increasingly resent their country's humbling reliance on the United States for defense. This is especially true among the country's younger generation, more worldly than their parents, with little or no memory of North Korea's invasion.

Yet recently, there has been an unexpected turn of events that has complicated this relationship further. The American superpower now finds that its own economic

---

*By the end of 2008, the United States plans to relocate the military base and its 6,000 troops outside of Seoul to Camp Humphreys in Pyongtaek. Koreans will then resume control of the land, which was headquarters of the occupying Imperial Japanese Army prior to the U.S. military's arrival. Seoul has not announced what will be built on the land, though a park or some other form of public use is likely.

security is increasingly intertwined with policy decisions going on behind closed doors in Seoul. In a small sense, at least, the mighty U.S. economy is even vulnerable to the actions of these South Korean policymakers.

South Korea's story offers the flipside to Ecuador's tale, though both illustrate how a globalized currency changed the rules with which countries interact with the world's top economic power. Ecuador, in choosing to become a dollar colony, has surrendered much of its financial independence to the United States in exchange for greater monetary stability. South Korea, by contrast, has usurped some of America's financial independence by accumulating massive dollar reserves. It is one of a handful of Asian countries, along with China and Japan, whose dollar war chest has made its central bank's every move closely watched by currency and government bond traders. Any sign that these countries are losing their appetite for dollars is considered potentially disastrous for the U.S. currency.

There's not much evidence to suggest that South Korean or other Asian officials had this in mind when they rapidly built up their foreign currency reserves. Seoul was simply trying to insulate its economy against another financial shock, like the one it suffered in the late 1990s. Nor is there any reason to believe that South Korea would be eager to exert this new power by trying to destabilize the dollar. After all, South Korea is an ally. More persuasively, the country owns so many dollars that such an act would likely be self-defeating: If South Korea sold dollars, sparking a broader sell-off in the currency, it would reduce the value of its own holdings and potentially destabilize its own economy. Yet, as former Treasury Secretary Lawrence Summers notes, one uncomfortable thought remains: The fate of the U.S. currency is now in foreign hands. That a group of foreign technocrats should hold such sway over the mighty dollar and, by extension, the U.S. economy is a modern development. It's a turn of events that shows that if the world's most important currency bestows many unique advantages, it can also bring unintended consequences.

*   *   *

In recent years, the dollar has faced off against a new boogeyman. It goes by the innocuous, even tedious, name of "central bank reserve diversification." But so much as a hint of it can send the value of the U.S. currency plunging. Central banks hold foreign currency reserves for the same reason that people keep fire extinguishers in their homes or spare tires in their cars: They want it there in case of an emergency, even if they hope they'll never need to use it. There is not a clear consensus about the appropriate level of foreign reserves, though most economists think the minimum should exceed a country's short-term foreign-currency debt.

Until recently, large foreign reserves have not characterized the Far East. Just the opposite is true. About twenty-five years ago, the so-called Asian Tigers began attracting worldwide attention for their booming development: Thailand, Malaysia, the Philippines, Indonesia, Singapore, South Korea, and others in the region grew their economies at startling rates of 8 percent to 12 percent between the mid-1980s and the early 1990s. The model was based on cheap labor and mass exports to the West. Much of the profits were funneled back into education and used to improve worker productivity. Economists at the time heralded this approach as a superior prototype— one where the private and public sectors worked in harmony to promote rapid industrialization and a better quality of life for a country's citizens.

At the same time, Asia's booming stock markets and relatively high interest rates attracted huge amounts of foreign capital and investors eager to finance—and profit from—the Asian economic miracle. With so much money pouring in, and with what seemed an unlimited ability to borrow more, high-flying Asian economies didn't spend much time worrying about foreign reserves, just as few drivers motoring along an interstate ever worry about the condition of their spare tire—that is, until they get a flat.

In 1997, the excesses of Asia's rapid economic growth came home to roost. Rising U.S. interest rates forced these countries to hike up their own already-high interest rates to continue attracting foreign capital. Their foreign currency debt levels rose and their current account deficits ballooned. These deficits caught the attention of currency speculators. Most Asian countries maintained monetary stability by allowing their currencies to trade only within a narrow range against the U.S. dollar. Now their currencies appeared vulnerable at a time when the foreign reserves they needed to defend these currencies looked dangerously low. The spare tire in the trunk, it turned out, was bald and ill-fitting, and the car veered off the road.

Asian stock and bond markets plunged as governments

across the region were forced to devalue their currencies. Companies went bankrupt and governments turned to the International Monetary Fund for emergency rescue packages worth billions of dollars. Thailand suffered first. The stock market tumbled 75 percent in 1997, and the currency, the baht, lost half its value versus the dollar between that July and January 1998. Not long after, the Philippines tried to defend its currency by jacking up the overnight bank rate from 15 percent to 24 percent. Its currency plummeted anyway, from 26 pesos to 40 pesos to the dollar in a period of a few months. The Malaysian overnight lending rate, the short-term rate at which banks lend to one another, soared to an eye-popping 40 percent in an effort to ward off speculators. It didn't work, but the exorbitant interest rate level choked the economy, causing it to contract by 6.2 percent in 1998. Malaysian industries most sensitive to interest rates were hit the hardest; the construction industry, for example, shrunk by more than 20 percent, leaving a plague of half-finished office buildings to dot the Kuala Lumpur skyline.

In Indonesia, companies that borrowed heavily in dollars found that debt much harder to pay back when the local currency, the rupiah, tumbled. Despite a $23 billion IMF loan, the currency and stock exchange hit new lows in September 1997, the country's bond rating was cut from investment-grade to junk (further raising the cost of borrowing dollars), the price of imported goods and food skyrocketed, and riots occurred across the country. Shops were looted and hundreds were left dead. By the following year, President Suharto was compelled to resign.

As South Koreans watched on in horror, few expected this financial "contagion" to spread as far north as Seoul.

After all, South Korea didn't share the same gaping current account or trade deficits as many of those other countries. Moreover, the size and strength of South Korea's economy distinguished it within the region: Its economy was the eleventh largest in the world and South Korea had recently been admitted to the Organization of Economic Cooperation and Development, making it the only Asian country besides Japan to belong to this elite club of democratic, free market nations.

Yet South Korea had an Achilles' heel: too much dollar debt that was due in the near-term and not enough in foreign reserves to convince creditors that it could make good on all those loans. So, in November, currency speculators turned their sights on Seoul. The Bank of Korea spent tens of billions of dollars in an effort to defend its sinking currency, but in a matter of weeks, the nation's reserves dwindled from around $30 billion to less than $5 billion.

South Korean officials enforced a narrow trading band for the won: The currency could rise or fall no more than 2.25 percent against the dollar in any daily session. But with Seoul's reserve tank running on empty, the speculators felt in control. They went on the attack the moment the trading day began, selling the South Korean currency relentlessly. In only five minutes at the start of each morning, the 2.25 percent limit would be reached, and the won would be done trading for the day. After several days of five-minute trading sessions, South Korea widened the trading band to 10 percent. This larger band made matters worse. It seemed to embolden the speculators, who smelled desperation and aimed to hit the 10 percent limit as quickly in the trading day as possible.

The situation was unsustainable. As with its neighbors in Southeast Asia, South Korea was eventually compelled to seek aid from the International Monetary Fund. Under the IMF's conditions for a $20 billion financial bailout, Seoul agreed to let its currency trade without any daily limits. The won's value weakened to 1,700 to the dollar from less than 1,000 before the crisis. In this bleak environment, many Korean companies were forced into mergers to survive or were sold off to foreigners. The least-attractive ones went bankrupt. So dire was the situation that the South Korean government nearly canceled the country's annual Lunar New Year celebration. The popular three-day holiday would cost the government about $1 billion in lost revenue from potential exports, and Seoul wasn't sure it could afford it. The festivities went ahead as planned, but only after officials called on the South Korean people for personal sacrifices to help fill the nation's empty reserve tank. Its patriotic citizens rose to the occasion. South Koreans contributed more than one hundred tons of gold—trinkets, family jewelry, even wedding rings—worth over $1 billion for the government to sell for foreign currency.

*   *   *

A common lesson of the Asian financial crisis was that these countries needed to boost their reserves. That would help insulate their economies from future speculative attacks and smooth out any market jitters. Most went at this task with vigor. By 2007, the six largest

Asian central banks boasted foreign currency reserves of more than $3 trillion—more than double the amount of foreign reserves held *worldwide* in 1995, according to the International Monetary Fund. About two-thirds of the total amount was held by the region's two giants: Japan, the world's second-largest economy, and China, the emerging economic superpower.

But the most remarkable foreign reserve growth over that period was in South Korea. Steadily accumulating dollars since succumbing to an IMF bailout, South Korea's foreign reserves ballooned to $110 billion by 2002, and by the end of 2006, that reserve figure had more than doubled. Today, the Bank of Korea, the central bank, boasts more than $250 billion in foreign currency holdings, most of them in dollars. That's the fifth-highest reserve total in the world, trailing only China, Japan, Russia, and Taiwan. After years of holding its currency steady versus the dollar, the Bank of Korea was happy to let the won fall to cheap levels against the U.S. currency to help boost South Korean exports. Like many of its Asian neighbors, the South Korean economy focuses on sales abroad, in particular to the United States, where it is often pitted directly against Chinese companies in industries ranging from shipbuilding and steel to computer memory chips. Since China keeps the yuan pegged to the dollar at what most analysts consider an undervalued level, the Bank of Korea felt it also had to keep the won cheap versus the dollar for South Korean exporters to remain globally competitive. This meant that South Korean officials would intervene frequently in the foreign exchange market, buying dollars and selling South Korean won, in an effort to keep the home currency cheap. The more exports to the United States, the more dollars the South Korean government adds to its growing stockpile.

This relationship holds some appeal to the United States, too, even if some members of Congress have been critical of China for keeping its currency from appreciating versus the dollar. As long as Asian governments keep their currencies weak, it means American consumers can buy goods made in Asia at discounted prices, from laptop computers and cell phones to sweatshirts and coffee tables. This keeps U.S. inflation subdued. Moreover, Asian governments plow most of the dollars they acquire from exports to the United States back into the U.S. Treasury market; their regular and robust purchases of government debt have kept bond yields near historically low levels. That not only means that the government can borrow cheaply, but that these low yields translate into low-interest-rate loans for the consumer on cars and home mortgages.

But the Bank of Korea's stockpiling of dollars did more than protect its currency from any future speculative attacks. The bulging reserve war chest, it turned out, endowed the central bank with the power to impact the $3-trillion-a-day foreign exchange market—and to make the mighty U.S. dollar quiver.

The financial world got a taste of South Korea's burgeoning power on February 22, 2005. Reports that day from foreign news correspondents based in South Korea said that the central bank planned to tell parliament it was preparing to diversify its foreign-exchange reserves. Since central banks worldwide hold on average about two-thirds of their foreign reserves in dollars, the term "diversification" has become a buzzword that currency traders tend to read as code for dumping dollars in favor of other currencies, like the euro or yen. Even worse, the news report raised fears that other Asian central banks might follow Seoul's lead and slow their purchases of dollar-denominated securities.

To many traders, such "diversification" made a lot of sense. The dollar was mired in a punishing three-year bear market that had caused its value against the euro to plunge by 50 percent and more than 20 percent against the yen and several other Asian currencies. As U.S. trade deficits and the country's debt relative to gross domestic product grew, sooner or later foreigners would become wary of holding more and more dollars. How long, these traders wondered, would central banks continue to store most of their precious reserves in a currency that looked poised to keep falling in value?

The market's response to the news report was swift and unsparing. The dollar tumbled not only against the won; it retreated against most every major currency worldwide. But the turmoil didn't end there. It raised all sorts of concerns that usually accompany a rapidly weakening currency—from talk of rising U.S. inflation and interest rates to an exodus of foreign investors who wouldn't want to hold American stocks and bonds if the dollar was to go into a serious bear market. Fears of a dollar meltdown spilled over to the U.S. stock and bond markets, leading the Dow Jones Industrial Average to its biggest one-day point decline in twenty-two months. On the New York Stock Exchange, declining stocks outpaced gainers by more than two to one on trading volume that was the heaviest of that year. The price of crude oil and gold, both of which tend to move in the opposite direction of the dollar, surged.

" 'Diversification' is not a word you want to hear if you hold dollars," Bob Prince at Bridgewater Associates, a giant Connecticut-based hedge fund, told *The Wall Street Journal* shortly after the market sell-off. "Since most central banks hold almost all of their reserves in U.S. dollars, diversification always means 'sell dollars and buy euros and yen.' "

In Seoul, government officials awoke the next morning in disbelief over what they saw. The Bank of Korea quickly issued a statement saying that the news report had misinterpreted the central bank's intentions. Diversification, the South Korean officials insisted, did not mean what some hedge fund managers like Prince suggested. The South Koreans said they meant moving some reserves out of low-yielding U.S. government bonds and into other, higher-yielding securities, such as corporate bonds or federal agency debt. But that didn't necessarily mean a move away from the dollar. In fact, South Korean officials said that the recent declines in the dollar would play no role in influencing their foreign reserve holdings, and they denied they had any near-term plans to sell dollars.

These calming words from South Korean bank officials did the trick. The dollar sell-off ended, and stock and bond markets around the world settled down. There would be no dollar fire sale after all. Someone in the media had just set off a smoke detector by mistake. Yet even after this false alarm, one thing had become painfully clear: South

Korea's massive dollar holdings conferred on this nation of fewer than 50 million people an awesome ability to cause the mighty U.S. economy to tremble. Such a turnabout in the dynamics of U.S.–South Korean relations was hardly something that either side could have expected. Indeed, in the history of currencies, it would be difficult to find another case where what de Gaulle had dubbed the "exorbitant privilege" could be turned on its head—in effect, relegating the superpower's financial well-being to the reserve management decisions of a much smaller ally.

Until recently, medium-sized economies like South Korea's had never amassed such a large stockpile of the world's main reserve currency. Asia's disastrous experiences during the financial crisis and the ensuing recommitment to boost economies through an even more intensive export-led growth strategy changed that. At the same time, the surge in oil prices to record levels has also elevated reserve holdings in Russia and the Middle East. So, the cumulative effect is that central banks—and in particular, Asian central banks—have become the last line of defense for the dollar.

"They are the buyers of last resort," said Brad Setser, an economist and fellow at the Council on Foreign Relations in New York. "During periods when private investors haven't been willing to add to their dollar holdings, the currency has come under pressure. But central banks, particularly in Asia, continued to intervene in the market to buy dollars and add to their U.S. Treasury holdings."

Most economists and analysts don't consider it likely that central banks will lose their appetite for dollar assets

anytime soon. They hoard U.S. government bonds because they are still considered the safest and most easily
tradeable securities around. The central banks of Asian
countries, moreover, may remain content to buy dollars
as long as these countries continue to rely on exports to
the United States as a main growth engine for their
economies.

Yet America's growing current account deficit (the
difference between what the United States earns abroad
and what it spends abroad) has raised concerns among
many economists and currency analysts. At around 7
percent of gross domestic product, the U.S. current account deficit is the highest ever for a major economy and
on par with the deficit levels of Thailand and Mexico before their crises. The United States is also the world's
largest debtor nation. It's true that people have been
worried about the size of this deficit for years and so far
the dollar has not suffered the sort of crash seen in
emerging markets. Unlike developing countries, the
United States borrows abroad in its own currency, so its
creditors don't have to worry if the United States has
enough dollars to repay the loans. Even so, some foreign
bank officials have expressed concern that U.S. imbalances
could one day cause a run on the dollar—and those with
the most dollars will feel the pain most acutely.

In China, which has an estimated $405 billion in U.S.
Treasury debt as of mid-2007, recent government state-
ments have raised the prospect of Beijing diversifying into
other currencies. "I think the Chinese government should
take some action to reduce . . . the accumulation of [dol-
lars] as we're still facing the possibility of a big devaluation
of the U.S. dollar," Yu Yongding, a member of the

People's Bank of China monetary policy committee, said in December 2005. "If that happens, it will be a tremendous hit to the Chinese economy." About a year later, Premier Wen Jiabao said that China will "strengthen the management of foreign-exchange reserves and actively explore and expand the channels and methods of using the reserves"—words many analysts interpreted as the beginning of a gradual move toward relatively fewer dollar reserves. Shortly after Wen's pronouncement, China revealed plans to move about $300 billion of its $1.2 trillion in foreign reserves to a separate fund that would be invested more aggressively and, presumably, not only in dollars.

· Russian finance officials have also had harsh words for the greenback. During a period in 2006 when the dollar was weakening regularly against both the Russian ruble and the euro, Russian finance minister Alexei Kudrin blasted the dollar as "unreliable as a reserve currency." His words were backed by deeds: Russia announced in 2006 that it held 50 percent of its reserves in currencies other than the dollar, compared with only 30 percent of its reserves in nondollar currencies as recently as 2004. There are also fresh signs that Middle Eastern nations, flush with petrodollars from rising oil prices, are becoming more skittish about the weakening greenback as they try to prevent their economies from overheating. Kuwait, in May 2007, said in order to fight inflation it was ending its currency's peg to the dollar.

Meanwhile, Asian central banks, from Taiwan and Singapore to China and Japan, might also worry about the deteriorating value of their own massive dollar reserves and would not want to be the last one to sell. In any event, these governments might feel more comfortable letting their currency appreciate against the dollar as long as they know that their Asian competitors are prepared to do the same. Some traders worry that if one central bank gets nervous about the prospects of the dollar and decides to reduce its dollar holdings, it could unleash a potentially dangerous chain reaction across the region.

Barry Eichengreen argues that Asian central banks engage in a sort of cartel-like behavior, where individual actions are tempered by group considerations. "It may be in their collective interest to hold dollars to keep their currencies down and the dollar up," he wrote, "but it is in their individual interest to get out before the bottom falls out of the U.S. currency."

It was this fear of a fast-moving ripple effect that made the possibility of South Korea selling dollars all the more frightening. Prince at Bridgewater said that if central banks were to suddenly stop accumulating dollars and investing in U.S. government debt, the fallout for the American economy and interest rates would be severe: U.S. bond yields would have to rise about 1.5 percentage points to attract private investor money to offset the lost central bank purchases.

A few months before the news report in Seoul spooked global markets, Lawrence Summers, Treasury secretary during the final two years of the Clinton administration, expressed his concerns about the U.S. reliance on Asian central banks to loan us money (which is what buying our government debt means) and to support the dollar. In an article for *Foreign Policy* magazine in 2004, he wrote, "The emerging economies of Asia, in particular, are actively accumulating claims on the United States by gobbling up U.S. Treasury bills, much as European states hoarded gold centuries ago. Much has been made of U.S. dependence on foreign energy, but the country's dependence on foreign cash is even more distressing."

* * *

Seoul today is a thoroughly modern metropolis. The capital city's 11 million citizens are fashion-forward, Internet-ready, and tireless. Decimated by the Japanese occupation and the invasion from North Korea during the first half of the twentieth century, Seoul has been almost entirely rebuilt, and its people continue to reinvent their city every few years. The central neighborhoods are a noisy collision of boxy skyscrapers, lean towers, traffic jams, smoky barbecue restaurants (and even smokier karaoke bars), blinking neon lights and jumbo outdoor video screens, strong-smelling food stalls, and gargantuan department stores that occupy entire blocks and rise several stories into the sky. Indeed, South Koreans love shopping so much—and typically work such long hours—that they can hunt for clothes and shoes by famous European or cutting-edge South Korean designers, toys, household goods, textiles, and more at the Dongdaemun market at almost any hour of the day. Its 30,000 shops don't close until 5:00 A.M.

A few minutes' drive from there is the Itaewon district, where its proximity to the American military base makes the neighborhood a playground for 8,000 GIs.

The main street is known for its sidewalk shops that sell made-to-measure suits, pyramids of luggage, long racks of leather jackets, Greek and Middle Eastern food, and du rag caps. Taxis crawl along with signs in the windows offering "Free Translation" (which is to say access to a cell phone with a knowledgeable English-speaker on the other end) because hardly any drivers speak or understand foreign languages. Girly bars on nearby "hooker hill" are not far from a giant KFC that does a brisk late-night business. Narrow alleyways lead to intimate lounge bars, rowdy English pubs, and casual French or Italian cafés, where a meal costs more than it would at the same sort of café in New York or Milan or Paris. It is around here that people stand on long lines on Saturday nights to use the handful of ATMs that accept foreign bankcards. Also in the area, hungry soldiers or expats can get an American-style brunch on Sunday morning. Not only will they find a hearty breakfast of bacon and eggs or pancakes with free refills of coffee, but it's one of the rare places in Asia where the stomach-busting-size portions will rival those served in American kitchens.

Compared to the pulsating neon and dense crowds found throughout the city, the area surrounding South Korea's central bank seems staid by comparison. The Bank of Korea is housed in one of the few buildings to survive the destruction inflicted by both the Japanese and the country's civil war. The gray structure, made of granite and capped with two domed roofs of steel, is modeled after a sixteenth-century French castle. Designed by the Japanese architect Tatsuno Kingo, it was completed in 1912 as a private bank. After South Korea's liberation in 1950, the building became home to the new country's fledgling central bank. In Seoul's ever-changing architectural landscape, the bank's office looks like it has been around since the European Renaissance, giving the impression of stability. And stability is what every central bank aims to project above all.

Heung-Sik Choo has had a hand in managing the Bank of Korea's foreign reserves for more than two decades. During most of his tenure, the job must have been pretty boring. It wouldn't have attracted South Korea's most ambitious, who understood that the real power in their society lay in securing an important post at one of the nation's elite conglomerates, known as *chaebols,* like Samsung or LG.

Choo doesn't look like one of those hard-charging types. He's short, slight of build, with thin-wired glasses and fine features. When I met him at the bank one drizzly September afternoon in 2006, he was wearing a plain blue sports coat, in marked contrast to the flashy designer suits favored by the better-known South Korean businessmen. In his lapel was a pin of the South Korean flag, reminiscent of U.S. politicians who wear a Stars and Stripes pin in their jacket lapels to boast of their patriotism. Although he spoke excellent, only slightly accented English—the result of an education at Michigan State University and his four years at the Bank of Korea's New York City branch office—he was so soft-spoken and shy that I had to lean in close to hear what he was saying.

Yet, make no mistake: These days, Choo's authority over where to invest the Bank of Korea's $250 billion in foreign currency reserves makes him a very significant man. It's an influence he's only recently started to recognize. "I was a little surprised," he said, nodding slowly as he recalled the magnitude of the global dollar sell-off that February day in 2005. It was the first time, he remembers, that questions over South Korea's foreign reserve management had such a commanding effect on the value of the dollar—and other markets—around the world.

For most of Choo's career, South Korea's foreign reserves attracted less attention on Wall Street than last night's Yankees' score or the daily lunch special at the cafeteria. And because the Bank of Korea's foreign reserve level was relatively small, the decision about where to park the reserves was easy. Choo held that money in the safest, most liquid (or easily convertible to cash) assets he could find. That was so these funds could be recalled quickly if needed to defend the currency from speculative attacks, like the one that brought South Korea to the brink of crisis at the end of 1997. That usually meant storing money in short-term U.S. Treasury bills and rolling those over regularly. Little of his personal discretion factored into the investment process; achieving a high return on the bank's investment was not a priority. Choo's job, to a certain degree, could be run on automatic pilot.

Now the rules are changing. As South Korea's reserves pile up, government officials are beginning to relax. They feel increasingly confident that the country holds more than enough in foreign currency to protect the won or to insulate the economy from any sudden exit of foreign capital. So the Bank of Korea is looking to invest some of its reserves more aggressively, shifting money that in the past would have gone toward T-bills into securities that offer a higher potential return, such as corporate bonds, mortgage-backed securities, or debt issued by federal agencies like Fannie Mae and Freddie Mac.

Analysts and foreign exchange traders are watching the Bank of Korea's moves closely. Many suspect that the dollar's recent weakness—the ballooning trade deficit and rising foreign debt level that are expected to keep the currency under pressure—is raising concerns in South Korea. Analysts wonder if these fears will lead to substantial reductions in the central bank's dollar holdings. But Choo isn't about to reveal his hand.

"It's true that as our reserves grow, we want higher returns," he told me in his office. "But that doesn't necessarily mean investing out of dollars. When you speak of diversification, you have to distinguish between currency diversification and asset diversification." The Bank of Korea doesn't disclose the percentage of its reserves held in dollars, but other South Korean finance officials acknowledge that "diversification" will inevitably include a gradual shift into other currencies.

"Yes, that's right," says Keehong Rhee, "it's even happening at the moment." Rhee should know. He's part of a new government organization known as the Korea Investment Corporation, or KIC. The KIC was created specifically to invest foreign currency reserves more aggressively than South Korea has ever done before. It is modeled after a similar fund used in Singapore, the Government Investment Corp. (GIC), and along with the GIC, the KIC is considered a prototype for the new investment fund being developed by China's central bank. It is part of a new breed of government-controlled funds in Asia and the Middle East, often referred to as sovereign wealth funds, designed to invest reserves more aggressively in search of higher returns. With a staff of forty-five people, the KIC was launched in 2006 with $20 billion to invest: $17 billion on behalf of the Bank of Korea and $3 billion for the Ministry of Finance and Economy.

Rhee is forty-six years old but still boyishly handsome, with a full head of jet-black hair and the compact build of a wrestler. He came to the KIC after many years of managing money for Samsung Life Insurance and then the giant U.K.–Hong Kong bank HSBC. From his sixteenth-floor perch in the shiny new Seoul Financial Center, visitors are afforded stunning panoramic views of the metropolis. As I learned, I wasn't the only one from the United States who had taken in that view recently. Over the past few months, Rhee volunteered, officials from the U.S. Treasury Department, Wall Street bankers, and representatives of Freddie Mac and Fannie Mae all passed through the KIC's mahogany doors. The impressive list of visitors testified to the importance of South Korea's massive dollar holdings. These personal appearances suggested that there was at least some question—perhaps even a little concern—about whether the KIC would share the Bank of Korea's traditional enthusiasm for U.S. assets. "The Treasury people wanted to make sure we still planned to buy Treasury debt," Rhee told me.

He assured them that the KIC didn't plan any radical change from the Bank of Korea's investment approach; in fact, his staff was in regular communication with Choo at the central bank. Like many South Koreans who came to the United States for their graduate education, Rhee is fluent in English. Yet he spoke slowly and chose his words carefully, as if to emphasize how deliberate and methodical his institution would be. Most of the KIC's investments, he continued, would closely mirror those already being made by the central bank. Both he and Choo would measure themselves against the same investment benchmark that emphasized U.S. bonds and other traditionally conservative investments.

Still, Rhee told me, some of the money entrusted to the KIC would indeed be invested more aggressively. That was the whole point. Over time, as the central bank and finance ministry allocated additional funds to the KIC, more and more money would be invested with an eye toward higher returns, he added. "We will go into riskier areas," Rhee said. "It is almost our duty."

He's not the only one who feels that way. Unlike the Federal Reserve or the European Central Bank, which turn tidy profits each year, the Bank of Korea has been *losing* money since 2004. Those losses are an unfortunate by-product of South Korea's currency policy. The government is a regular buyer of dollars and seller of won to keep the local currency relatively cheap, which helps make South Korean goods more globally competitive. But despite Seoul's intervention, the won appreciated by 28 percent against the dollar from 2004 to 2006. That made the value of the central bank's dollar holdings worth that much less in the local currency.

Another factor that hurt the central bank's bottom line is low U.S. interest rates. Unlike China or Japan, South Korea's interest rates for a while have been higher than those in the United States. That means when the Bank of Korea sold bonds denominated in won and then invested those proceeds in lower-yielding U.S. government bonds, it lost money with each transaction. This combination of lower U.S. rates and a weakening dollar relative to the won tipped the bank's balance sheet into the red. As a consequence, I was told during my visit to Seoul, the Bank of Korea had made no contribution to the government treasury for the past three years. "Korea has felt the pain of reserve accumulation more acutely than Japan or China," Setser said.

Choo says that while the bank's losses have been tolerated, they have not gone unnoticed by the South Korean parliament. "We are getting more pressure than before to boost the returns on foreign exchange reserves," he said. The lawmakers' mood has changed from even a few years ago. In the aftermath of South Korea's financial crisis, the country was of one mind: Seoul needed to rebuild its foreign currency reserves as rapidly as possible, and these reserves should be kept readily available to defend the currency and cover South Korea's foreign debt. By the end of 2001, foreign reserves had topped the $100 billion mark, more than easily covering the country's external short-term debt.

With that figure now at around $250 billion, parliament has begun clamoring for the Bank of Korea to invest its reserves more aggressively to make up that shortfall on the central bank's balance sheet. Some of South Korea's parliament members even envision profits from more aggressive central bank investing helping fund state projects. These motivations led to the creation of the KIC and its mandate for seeking better returns. "This is our national wealth," Rhee put it. "We want to increase that wealth."

When the dollar was appreciating against the won, investing reserves in U.S. assets meant that the strong dollar boosted South Korea's returns when translated back to the local currency. But with the dollar now falling steadily against the won, how much longer before South Korea shifts an increasing amount of its reserves into non-dollar assets? Additional pressure on the central bank to return to profitability makes such a shift more tempting.

South Koreans, however, are not the only ones in Asia reconsidering how to invest these holdings. "The secular trend is greater diversification," Edward Robinson from the Monetary Authority of Singapore told me in an interview at his office in October 2005. As the executive director for economic policy for Singapore's central bank, he helps influence investment decisions for the city-state's $150 billion in foreign currency holdings. Like South Korea, Singapore doesn't disclose what percentage of its reserves are held in dollars. But Robinson said that the introduction of the euro in 1999 offered a "viable alternative" to the dollar that hadn't existed since the dollar assumed the role of the primary world reserve currency. "The Japanese economy seems to be picking up," he added. "I think the yen will become increasingly important and a lot more attractive."

Still, not everyone thinks the diversification issue should be a big concern for the dollar. Jeffrey Young, a former currency analyst at Citigroup in New York, said that, contrary to popular perception, central banks usually *don't* sell the dollar when its value is slipping. In fact, he said, data from the IMF show just the opposite. Like most other investors, governments prefer to buy low and sell high. "Central banks increase their share of dollars in new reserves when the dollar is weak and decrease the dollar share when the currency is strong." This suggests that central banks are keen to diversify their holdings into other currencies. But as Rhee says, they wish to do so only gradually—in a way that doesn't impact the dollar's value and the worth of their own portfolios. "It would take a very large shock to confidence in the dollar, such as would be delivered by a lurch to protectionism in the U.S., or a sudden upsurge in inflation, in order to trigger a sharp decline in the dollar share of official reserves," Young said.

A bias toward dollars may be harder to kick for other, more intangible reasons. The average South Korean is still used to viewing the outside world in terms of dollars. The elite in South Korea send their children to the United States for college or graduate school or jobs at American companies. As a result, "many Koreans have dollar liabilities," Choo notes. They know how much a New York or Los Angeles apartment costs in dollars. But the average South Korean would have little idea what most things cost in euros. "Korean people know the dollar as a method of payment," Rhee says. "Historically, it is what they have had the most confidence in."

And yet that mentality may be changing. Rhee told me that five or ten years ago, the elderly ladies who deal currency on the street as part of Seoul's black market did the bulk of their business by offering dollars in exchange for won. Today, Rhee said, the same grandmothers who do most of these unofficial transactions find fewer customers for the world's primary reserve currency than for China's yuan. "People think that's now the currency to own, the one that's going to appreciate," Rhee said. Meanwhile, Choo says the growing U.S. deficits and predictions of long-term dollar declines are constant conversation fodder among South Koreans. "There is some concern," he acknowledges. "These stories aren't necessarily based on serious research. But you read about it in newspaper articles."

* * *

Remarkably, less than three months after the news reports about the Bank of Korea rocked the financial world, something quite similar happened again. This time it was a story in the *Financial Times* that quoted then–governor of the Bank of Korea Park Seung saying that the government would no longer intervene in the foreign exchange market. Currency traders took that to mean that the central bank was prepared to sit back and let the market dictate the value of the won. Given South Korea's large trade surplus with the United States and its perceived undervalued currency, that almost certainly would equate to a big won rally. The won and most other Asian currencies that day rallied hard against the dollar.

It turned out to be another false alarm. South Korean officials needed only a few hours to deny the report this second time. They said the governor's comments had been "distorted"—though the *Financial Times* said it stood by its story—and that the central bank would be "ready to act whenever the currency market is unstable." Not content with the statement alone, the Bank of Korea then actively sold won and bought dollars during the next day's trading. The dollar, after a powerful sell-off following the *Financial Times* article, snapped back to erase those earlier losses, just as it had in February.

When the blizzard of trading subsided and heartbeats returned to normal, many traders with the benefit of hindsight expressed some skepticism about the story.

Preventing the won from appreciating—or at least from appreciating too rapidly—was integral to South Korea's export-led growth strategy. Why would the government suddenly do an about-face regarding its policy on currency intervention? And even if this happened to be true, why would the government ever announce this change to the media? The news would surely destabilize financial markets, and besides, governments rarely, if ever, tip their hands like that.

But beyond dispute was how jittery the currency market had become. Traders proved eager to sell dollars on even the slightest sign that a major central bank had lost some of its dollar appetite. The won's second wild day of trading suggests that traders didn't view the first incident as a mere fluke. Many seemed to suspect it was only a matter of time until South Korea, and perhaps other Asian countries, had a change of heart about the role of the dollar in its foreign reserves. Now that Asian central banks had become such important global players, Americans faced a new reality: The stability of the almighty dollar could be propped up or brought down by countries that are already reassessing whether holding so many dollars is still in their best interest.

Paul Volcker, the former chairman of the Federal Reserve, does not see this relationship as stable over the long term. "Why are so many people willing to hold dollars with a bulging current account deficit, growing debt, and a country living beyond its means?" he wondered aloud when we met in his New York office during the fall of 2006. "You have to ask how long this state of affairs will last." And when it's over, Volcker added, you have to worry about what will happen to the dollar.

CHAPTER 6

An End to America's

Exorbitant Privilege?

*There is no subtler, no surer means of overturning
the existing basis of society than to debauch the
currency.*
—JOHN MAYNARD KEYNES,
The Economic Consequences of Peace

The World Money Show takes place each February at the Gaylord Palms Resort in Orlando,
Florida, a bustling, sixty-three-acre hotel and conven-
tion center that's five minutes from Walt Disney World.
But for the thousands of people who flock here every
winter, the Gaylord Palms has a carnival-like atmosphere all its own. The attendees, dressed casually in
khaki pants and brightly colored shirts, are primarily
upper-middle-class couples. Most are recently retired or
at least are approaching the day they can no longer
count on regular paychecks. They come to Orlando in
search of an innovative way to grow their savings, and
the 2006 show offered them plenty of advice on that. It
featured 206 companies from 39 countries, a labyrinth
of 261 booths and 330 individual workshops—all of it

crammed into a furiously paced four-day investment circus.

Under the Gaylord Palms's big tent, every hot theme and madcap idea-of-the-moment was on proud display: oil and gas futures trading, precious metal funds, real estate investment trusts, and so on. One man lectured on how to make money in Canadian utilities. Someone from Privatfinanz shared his picks for the hottest stocks in Germany. A representative from an outfit called Optionetics drew curious crowds to hear his "delta neutral trading" method. Jim Trippon, publisher of the just-launched China Stock Digest, offered a quick history lesson to a standing-room-only crowd. "Deng Xiaoping said it was glorious to get rich," he beamed, his voice rising so that those who spilled outside the Tallahassee Ballroom could hear. "I agree!"

Not far away, Chuck Butler was preparing his presentation. At fifty-two years old, Butler is a quiet, almost shy man, plain as hamburger. What he was serving up to the hungry crowds sounded pretty bland, too: savings accounts and certificates of deposit. Just a few minutes later, however, during his presentation, it became clear that Butler was promoting an idea more challenging than most anything else seen at the World Money Show. Butler's products were denominated in foreign currencies, and he was there to preach about threats to the dollar's reign as the world's top currency.

As the president of EverBank World Markets, an online bank based in St. Louis, Butler has spent much of the past two decades trying to convince anyone who would listen of the dollar's inevitable decline: a victim, as he sees it, of exploding deficits and too many greenbacks circulating the world. He advises Americans to put a chunk of their savings with EverBank—they offer savings accounts and CDs in twenty foreign currencies, including the euro, the yen, and the Chinese yuan—to protect themselves from the dollar's eventual comeuppance.

Many of the World Money Show's presenters were after a quick buck, offering schemes that would be forgotten by the next bull market. But Butler has grander ideas. He sees himself as a financial pioneer, hoping to popularize foreign-currency accounts the way Fidelity's Peter Lynch popularized the now ubiquitous mutual fund. Like Lynch, Butler dresses modestly and speaks in simple adages that the average investor can understand. He envisions the day when Americans will look back and shake their heads whenever they recall how they kept their money in a single currency. "You wouldn't put all your money in one stock, would you?" he put it to me. "Why keep it all in just one currency?"

Butler probably spends as much time thinking and talking about the dollar's future as anyone. But he's not the only person growing concerned. His words echo what economists—on Wall Street, at the World Bank, and even at the Federal Reserve (in the person of former chairman Alan Greenspan)—have warned: America's widening trade deficit and expanding foreign debt threaten to erode world confidence in the dollar. It may, in fact, already be happening. These analysts warn that in the event that central banks and other foreign creditors ever curb their appetite for the U.S. currency and stop funding this deficit, confidence could erode rapidly. Even if such an event never happens, many expect a gradual, grinding dollar decline to continue for years. In a world where the euro now offers the first genuine competition to the dollar in half a century, and with China's influence and financial power on the rise, some think the days of the dollar's dominance as the undisputed heavyweight champion of the currency world are coming to an end.

Among the wary is famed investor Warren Buffett, chief executive of Berkshire Hathaway. He told his clients in a 2004 shareholder letter that the firm was stepping up investments abroad over fears of the dollar. "Our country's trade practices are weighing down the dollar," Buffett wrote. "The decline in its value has already been substantial, but is nevertheless likely to continue." If he's right, it will be more than just dollar savings accounts that suffer. Americans enjoy daily benefits because of the dollar's role as the grease for global capitalism, from lower mortgage rates for families to cheap acquisitions abroad for companies. Washington is able to fund its large deficits through ever-expanding loans from foreign governments. The ramifications of losing this status following a collapse in the dollar are hard to know for sure, but the consequences could be dire.

"Losing reserve currency status will lead to a series of economic and political crises in the United States," says Avinash Persaud, president of Intelligence Capital Ltd., a London-based financial advisory firm, and the former global head of foreign exchange at JPMorgan. "This is something we know a lot about from the United Kingdom's experience. Having the reserve currency status is like being able to write check after check and not have anyone cash them. But when you lose the reserve currency status, it's as if all those checks are taken out from under the mattress, and suddenly cashed."

It may not be as simple as that, however. Before the dollar loses its crown, there has to be a new contender for the throne. Right now, no other currency looks quite up to the job. Not the British pound, whose best days are behind it. Not the Chinese yuan, whose world reserve status is decades away, if indeed it ever comes. Not even the euro, which offers the greatest challenge to the dollar but has problems of its own. What may happen instead is a continued weakening of the dollar with no substitute to take its place. That would make life harder for Americans, but it could take a toll on the world economy, too.

* * *

EverBank's headquarters are far from the hustle and bustle of trading floors in New York and London. The building is even several miles outside of St. Louis's modest financial district, located in a quiet suburban corner of the city, next to a Best Buy electronics store and a Sports Authority outlet. Butler arrives here each morning at 4:30 A.M. to an empty building and begins trading currencies during London hours. It's still dark outside when he enters his office, and Butler likes to keep it dim inside, too, preferring to tap out his daily commentary by the soft glow of his computer screen. "I like the serenity of the low lights," he explains. "For me, it's the best part of the day."

One blustery January morning in 2007, Butler is preparing his regular commentary, the *Daily Pfennig,*

EverBank's five-times-a-week currency market analysis that takes its name from the old German penny. Butler reads newspapers, websites, and, in his spare time, books with opportunistic titles like *The Coming Collapse of the Dollar and How to Profit from It*. But over the years, he has also built a roster of currency traders and other insider-figures around the world whom he consults. At a conference in Los Angeles several years ago, he even met the head of the New Zealand central bank, Donald Brash. The two hit it off and Brash invited the American to call him if he ever had questions about New Zealand's monetary policy. Butler gladly did so—and continued to do so even after Brash left the central bank and became a leader in the country's parliament.

Part of Butler's job is running the trader lingo and economist jargon through an easy-to-digest filter. This morning, he's focused on the pound. In recent weeks, the British currency has been at fourteen-year highs versus the dollar, aided earlier in the month by the Bank of England's interest rate increase. But comments the day before made by Bank of England governor Mervyn King raised questions about whether the central bank was done with its rate hikes. That perception was weakening the pound. Perpetually bearish on the dollar, Butler was having none of it. He gave his *Daily Pfennig* readers his opinion in the plainspoken language of his Missouri up-bringing: "Here's the skinny . . . When Mr. King decided to talk about inflation falling, it led traders to believe that he was saying that interest rate hikes would come to an end. . . . I think he bit off more than he can chew with that statement, and I wouldn't be too surprised if the 'spin doctors' in the U.K. can get him back

out there with a follow up statement that 'fixes' the inflation one."

This commentary is e-mailed to 22,000 people every
trading day, and it's posted on two financial websites—
where they receive about 250,000 page hits per day. The
Daily Pfennig generates on average one hundred responses per issue, Butler says, and he answers them all.
Some EverBank customers are wealthy individuals, globe-
trotters who want to have a euro account at the ready for
impromptu trips to the Côte d'Azur or small business
owners whose operations involve multiple currencies.
Others believe in the diversification benefits of spreading
their savings across a variety of assets and currencies.

Yet many EverBank clients have no practical use for
foreign currency. Rather, they share Butler's sense of
foreboding about the dollar's future. The super-rich, of
course, have always kept money abroad as a safety pre-
caution, even when the dollar's pre-eminence was not in
doubt. EverBank clients include many middle-class families who have read stories in the paper or seen commentary
on TV raising questions about the dollar's vulnerability.
They represent a small but growing movement of Americans who are already preparing for the day when the dollar
is no longer the only game in town.

Butler says more than 25,000 people in all fifty states
have opened up foreign currency accounts with the bank.
With a minimum investment of $2,500, anyone can open
a foreign currency savings account. With at least $10,000,
someone can buy a three-month to twelve-month foreign
currency CD, which, unlike the savings accounts, pays interest that reflects the country's local rates. That's negligi-
ble for yen certificates of deposit, since Japanese interest

rates are next to nothing, but significant in places like Iceland, where an Icelandic krona CD has paid an annual interest rate of 13 percent.

Oddly enough, Butler's interest in currencies began in early 1985—at a time when the dollar was still riding high. He had recently completed a finance degree at St. Louis Community College at Meramec, and he stayed in town to work as a bond trader for Mark Twain Bank. Butler soon noticed that many of his institutional clients were making big purchases of foreign bonds. Government bonds were considered the best way to play foreign currencies, and these investors believed the dollar's bull run of the 1980s couldn't continue much longer (sure enough, later that year, the major economic powers engineered a dollar devaluation with the Plaza Accord). Butler wanted to find a way for retail investors to protect themselves from potential dollar declines, too, but individuals weren't able to buy foreign government bonds. Foreign bond mutual funds were hard to come by back then. However, Butler had an inspiration: offer clients the ability to own the actual currencies themselves. So Mark Twain Bank made available about two dozen different currency accounts and CDs, a program Butler would continue when EverBank acquired the foreign currency operations of Mark Twain Bank in 2000.

The afternoon of his presentation at the Gaylord Palms in 2006, Butler made his pitch before an audience of about one hundred people spread throughout a half-filled auditorium. By a show of hands, some in the crowd indicated that they already had EverBank foreign currency accounts and that they were regular readers of the *Daily Pfennig*. Butler, a squat man with bright blue eyes that blink constantly, wore a loose-fitting blue sports jacket, khaki pants, and brown loafers. He looks a bit like George Costanza from the television show *Seinfeld*. Although Butler has a mild Midwestern twang instead of George's rough outer borough accent, he shares some of the television character's self-deprecation.

"I didn't tell you any lies about how I looked," Mr. Butler said flatly, beginning to pace. He was now addressing *Daily Pfennig* readers in the crowd who were seeing him in person for the first time. "I'm short. I'm overweight. I'm bald. I'm lucky my wife married me." Some in the audience began to chuckle. But Butler, now confident that these frank admissions had established his credibility as a straight-talker, warmed to his favorite subject. The conference was taking place a month after the dollar ended a three-year losing streak, from 2002 to 2004, during which the greenback lost 50 percent of its value to the euro. The sudden dollar rally in 2005—fueled by rising U.S. interest rates and the repatriation of profits by American companies exploiting a temporary tax break—caught most every analyst off guard. For the moment, at least, that dollar rebound took some wind out of the doomsayers' arguments. But Butler was here to caution that the large trade and budget deficits that pressured the currency earlier this decade still needed to be accounted for. "The financial stress and fundamental problems still exist," he warned.

Following the presentation, a small crowd of people approached Butler to get more information. Several said they planned to open savings accounts or buy some high-yielding foreign CDs. Butler didn't have to worry much that these customers might go to another bank. For

Americans interested in foreign currency accounts, there aren't many other places they can turn. Big national outfits like JPMorgan Chase and Wachovia don't offer these foreign currency accounts. Citibank did for about a dozen years but discontinued the service a few years ago, citing a lack of demand. It isn't hard to guess why. When the dollar was riding high from the mid-1990s to 2001, bolstered by strong economic growth and large flows of foreign money into the U.S. stocks, few Americans looked to invest abroad or worried about dollar depreciation.

But after the stock market bubble burst and following the terrorist attacks of September 11, currency traders became less sanguine about the U.S. economy and turned their focus to the gaping deficits. When the Federal Reserve cut interest rates, that further weighed on the dollar. Meanwhile, corporate titans like Buffett and Microsoft founder Bill Gates were publicly voicing their concern that America's growing economic imbalances signaled a long, potentially harrowing dollar decline. CNBC began airing slightly alarming stories on the falling dollar and whether the slump would result in a dollar crisis. In March 2005, *Newsweek* magazine ran a cover story with the title "The Incredible Shrinking Dollar." "The greenback's fall is stoking fears of a global crisis," the magazine proclaimed. All of which was great for Butler's business. In 2002, EverBank's foreign currency accounts had the equivalent of $132 million in assets. By 2006, that figure had risen to $1 billion.

Not everyone is sold on foreign currency accounts. Many financial advisors think foreign exchange movements are too hard to predict for the professionals—and far too risky for individuals to worry about. Yet some prominent dollar skeptics think that having at least a modest portion of one's savings in foreign currency accounts is a good idea. One such skeptic is Jim Rogers, a billionaire private investor, the former partner of hedge fund guru George Soros and the author of several best-selling books on global investing, including *Adventure Capitalist*. He is also an EverBank customer. Rogers expects the dollar to lose value for many years to come and views these accounts as a way to protect one's life's savings. "Everyone should have one," he says of the foreign currency accounts. "The rich, the poor, and the middle class."

As Butler sees it, the dollar is a victim of its own— and America's—success. Global demand for dollars leads us to print more, global confidence in the United States leads foreigners to snap up more Treasury bonds, and a strong economy that is open to the rest of the world leads American consumers to buy many foreign products. The result is growing indebtedness to foreigners, which means an ever-rising percentage of American GDP has to go toward financing interest payments owed to foreign lenders. This vulnerability to the currency preferences of foreign creditors has raised a question not heard much since the 1970s: Is the dollar's role at the center of the global economy no longer assured?

. . .

The introduction of the euro was a landmark day. At midnight, January 1, 1999, revelers across Europe celebrated not only the birth of a new year but of a new currency. News photos the next morning showed well-heeled people toasting the new year in hats and masks shaped in the now-familiar euro logo of a C with two parallel lines through its middle. They looked drunk on champagne—and perhaps on the anticipated power of their new currency, too. The euro replaced currencies used in eleven European nations known as the eurozone (Greece joined in 2001 and Slovenia in 2007 to bring the total to thirteen). It was set at a rate of 1.18 to $1. Never mind that the euro began life as merely an accounting currency and that the physical paper and coins were still three years away. Forget that, after an initial gain against the dollar in trading, the euro's value would soon plummet below parity and spend months worth less than 90 U.S. cents before it would rally again. Those were mere details. Europe had created something absent since World War II: a currency that was widely considered a credible alternative to the dollar.

Proponents of this view emphasize the size of Europe's currency union. Already 317 million Europeans count the euro as their currency—a number that slightly exceeds the population of the United States. Eleven more countries are poised to adopt the euro over the next several years. The European Union (which comprises twenty-seven member states, including some, most notably the United Kingdom, that have not committed to the euro) also accounts for a greater percentage of world output and global trade than does the United States. Many prominent U.S. economists predict that these advantages offer the foundation for a euro challenge to the dollar for world supremacy.

C. Fred Bergsten, a former U.S. Treasury assistant secretary for international affairs and a founding director at the Peterson Institute for International Economics, a highly regarded Washington think tank, has been perhaps the most outspoken booster of the euro. He's predicted that as much as $1 trillion of international investment could shift from dollars to euros. Among central bank reserves, this transition is already under way. In 1999, about 71 percent of world reserves were held in dollars and 18 percent in euros. By 2006, the dollar figure had fallen to 66 percent, while the euro reserve total rose to 25 percent. In other areas of global finance, the new currency has started to level the playing field between the United States and Europe. The euro helped unify Europe's capital markets, enabling European companies to raise money more cheaply and allowing Europe's bond markets to compete with America's. Today, the number of new issues and the money raised by bonds denominated in euros is now on par with those denominated in dollars. "For the first time in 50 years, investors have the stable currency of a comparable economic giant as an alternative to the dollar," Ewe-Ghee Lim, author of an International Monetary Fund working paper on the euro's challenge to the dollar, wrote in 2006.

Yet, that's not the same as saying the euro will ever displace the dollar, and the IMF report stops short of suggesting that. There are many reasons to believe that it may never seriously rival the U.S. currency for the top spot.

The euro faces potential obstacles all its own. To begin with, it's not even clear that Europeans want to spread the use of the euro throughout the world. Germany and France are the driving forces behind the development of the European Union and the common currency. But historically they have held opposing views on the benefits of a currency's use abroad. Germans tended to frown on a global role for the Deutsche mark because they felt it would complicate the ability to manage their own monetary policy. The French, meanwhile, saw a widely used currency as a means for exerting global influence. The European Central Bank (ECB) has tried to accommodate both views with a neutral approach. "When the euro was introduced, the ECB said it would neither encourage nor discourage its use around the globe," Lex Hoogduin, an economist, a former head of research at the Dutch central bank, and an advisor to the president of the ECB for four years said to me. "But clearly there are some at the ECB who don't advocate a global role for the euro."

Within the eurozone itself, there are large swaths of the population that have expressed doubts about the new currency. Some even hotly oppose it. To many critics, the problem is the European Central Bank, which sets interest rates for all thirteen member states. This one-size-fits-all monetary policy means that rates will almost always be inappropriate for some of the European countries, since economic growth can vary widely. Recently, ECB interest rates have been between 3 percent and 4 percent. That's seen as too high and punishing for slowing economies, like Italy's; at the same time, these levels are viewed as too low and overstimulative for economies worried about rising inflation, as the case has been with Ireland. For the ECB, one-size-fits-none may be a more accurate description.

The recent strength of the euro has also been behind an occasional populist backlash against the currency in several European countries. In June 2005, the former Italian welfare minister Roberto Maroni went so far as to call for a return of the Italian lira. The minister blamed the country's economic woes on the ECB's reluctance to lower interest rates. The euro had recently been near an all-time high versus the dollar, and that currency strength was taking a toll on Italian exporters. Italy's footwear, clothing, and furniture manufacturers compete directly with Chinese companies, where the currency is pegged to the dollar. So the euro's rapid appreciation made the Chinese goods even less expensive by comparison and, in some cases, priced Italian goods out of foreign markets. Italy's world-famous shoe production has been dropping steadily since the introduction of the euro, and in 2004, the country imported more shoes than it exported for the first time. Rossano Soldini, head of a family owned shoe factory in Capolona, a small Tuscan village, complained in 2005 that the euro was like "wearing handcuffs" and said that he pined for the old lira.

Maroni's controversial statement drew criticism from EU officials and even other Italian politicians, who said that the costs associated with leaving the euro would be worse than the sacrifices required for maintaining the currency union. But his comments came at the same time that other Europeans were turning against the idea of a more tightly knit union. Voters in France and the Netherlands rejected a proposed European Constitution that was intended to further integrate the countries politically, and the Italian welfare minister's remarks coincided with the release of a German magazine poll that showed that 56 percent of respondents wanted a return of the mark. In November 2006, a French magazine poll sounded even more hostile to the euro: It found that 52 percent of France regarded the euro as a "bad thing" and that 71 percent of

French blue-collar workers felt the euro had hurt them personally, blaming the new currency for price increases and job losses. A quarter of those polled said they still thought in terms of francs when shopping. The French survey was particularly stinging to euro-enthusiasts since, from the start, Paris was the main driver of a common European currency.

"I believe these economic strains will intensify over time," Robert Prior-Wandesforde, an economist with HSBC, told me in a 2006 interview. "The current path is unsustainable." Aside from Europe's internal squabbling over interest rates, Wandesforde says that Europe's demographics are a growing concern. Most European countries are aging and have restrictive immigration policies they would need to change to offset the increasing number of retirees. Without a policy shakeup, the net result would be shrinking populations that put pressure on the European economies. These pressures, former EU commissioner Frits Bolkestein said, will force some countries to borrow more money to meet their obligations to the swelling ranks of senior citizens. This in turn will increase budget deficits and cause interest rates to rise. The European economies hardest hit would demand the relief of interest-rate cuts. But their fate would be hostage to ECB technocrats in Frankfurt, and some countries might threaten to leave the European Union if rates didn't fall, Bolkestein suggested. "Therefore," the Dutch politician said in early 2006, "the long-term chances of survival of the euro should be questioned."

This sort of fatalistic view on the European Monetary Union remains a minority opinion. There are plenty of disincentives for Italy, or any other ambivalent country, to flee the EMU. Once out of the eurozone, a nation would face a sharp rise in interest rates on its public debt that could lead to higher taxes, a recession, and a slew of other unforeseen problems. It's not even clear how a country would revert back to its former currency, since the EU has never bothered to set up such a process. Most skeptics like Wandesforde still think the EMU can fix its problems and make the system satisfactory to all members. But he also thinks the weight of these troubles will discourage global adoption of the currency. "I struggle to see the euro ever replacing the dollar as the main world reserve currency," he summed up.

Others, like Persaud of Intelligence Capital Ltd., see China's yuan eventually succeeding where the euro will fail in challenging the dollar. This view, too, focuses on economic size and strength. Just as the dollar was destined to overtake the pound as the U.S. economy became the largest and most dynamic in the world, the reasoning goes, the yuan will become the global standard when China inevitably becomes the world's economic heavyweight and largest trading nation. There is merit to this argument, though such a transition is still purely speculative and remains probably decades away. It would require China's capital markets to mature and open up to foreign investment as the U.S. and European markets have done.

Some Pacific Rim countries are not waiting that long. Led by Japan, South Korea, and some of the Southeast Asian states, they are exploring the idea of a regional currency, known as the Asian Currency Unit. Modeled on the euro, the common Asian currency is part of a broader effort aimed at greater regional cooperation, including further development of local bond markets. So far, though, there has been little enthusiasm for a pan-Asian currency outside of the region. Economists note that the euro took decades to develop, and the differences in economic and political development are far wider in Asia than they are among the eurozone countries. Cooperation between China and Japan could prove even more daunting than that between longtime adversaries Germany and France. The two European powers had something to offer each other to bring about monetary union. France saw the euro as a means to extend its own global influence, while Germany decided that forgoing the mark was an acceptable price for its neighbor's acceptance of reunification. It's hard to imagine a similar quid pro quo developing between Japan and China that would lead either of these countries to forfeit use of its currency.

There's another reason why Asian countries may feel less urgency to create a new currency union: These nations already have a currency used throughout the region for international trade. It's called the U.S. dollar, and it has played a big part of Asia's rapid development over the past three decades by facilitating transactions across borders. "There is no alternative to the dollar as a trading currency in Asia," said Andy Xie, a Hong Kong–based economist and former head of Morgan Stanley's Asia Pacific economics group. "Eventually, the renminbi [yuan] will replace the dollar in Asia, perhaps in our lifetime. But it will take at least thirty to forty years."

Economists think it may take that long in part because the dollar's widespread use has generated a virtuous cycle that reinforces its leading status. This may be the most powerful reason why the dollar is so hard to displace. Some have compared the dollar's position to that of the Microsoft Windows operating system. Computer users may believe that competing software is easier to use or superior in other ways, but the convenience of being able to transfer files around the world to anyone using Microsoft makes the system attractive. In the foreign exchange world, widespread use of the dollar makes transacting in the currency easier and less expensive than any other. "The more countries that deal in dollars, the cheaper it is for them all to deal in dollars," Ronald McKinnon, the Stanford professor, says. In other words, any one country would be hesitant to stop transacting in dollars, even if it preferred to use a different currency, unless it knew that other countries would do the same.

Yet, even if no currency looks poised to knock the dollar off its mantel, that doesn't mean the euro and eventually the yuan or an Asian regional currency won't chip away at the dollar's dominance. The U.S. government could try to slow this erosion with policies aimed at encouraging American savings and reducing the bloated trade deficit. It could intensify the dollar's decline by enacting protectionist legislation that reduces U.S. international trade. But no matter what it does, some slippage in the dollar's status will be difficult to staunch. The global economy has changed too much since Bretton Woods officially made the dollar the free world's currency—or even since the 1990s, when the dollar faced no competition.

Today, Russia, the Baltic countries, and some countries in the Middle East readily embrace the euro, and not just at the central bank reserve level. People in these places are using the euro to pay for dinner in Michelin-starred restaurants, to get past the bouncers at velvet-roped nightclubs, and to stuff under their mattresses. All these functions a few years ago would have been satisfied with dollars. Their switch to the euro is not a reflection of the dollar's weakened value in the foreign exchange market. Rather, it is that countries within Europe's geographic and political sphere of influence have become converts to the euro because of that influence and trade with the continent. Even if the United States eliminates its trade deficit and the dollar's value soars again versus the euro, those inroads made by the new European currency are unlikely to reverse.

With the euro as a new rival, and another one potentially brewing in China, the dollar is unlikely ever to command the same global market share it did in the post–Cold War 1990s, when there was no genuine competitor in sight and America enjoyed unrivaled authority as the winner of the Cold War and the unchallenged superpower. So, if the dollar's spot on top of the mountain looks relatively secure, the distance between the mountaintop and its major rivals looks to be narrowing. Some economists see the world eventually dividing into three currency blocs: one using the yuan, one the euro, and one the dollar, each within a sphere of influence of a regional power. Professor Barry Eichengreen recently wrote, "There is no reason why, several decades from now, two or three reserve currencies cannot share the market, not unlike the situation before 1914" (when use of the pound was waning and demand for the dollar rising).

*   *   *

Chuck Butler has found out from bitter experience that proclaiming to Americans their currency is in a period of secular decline is not something most want to hear. This message has been met with threatening e-mails and even blustery talk of harm from some listeners at his conference presentations. The most common accusation, he says, is for the offended party to call into question Butler's patriotism. That hurts him more than being told that his analysis is poor or that he's a fool. "I tell them I'm one of the most patriotic Americans in the world," Butler complained. "But you can't confuse patriotism with investing your life savings."

He shouldn't have been surprised, though. Most countries take pride in their currencies, and Americans more so. After all, the dollar is one of the country's greatest success stories—the underpinning of the nation's financial might and a powerful source of global influence.

Few understood this better than French president de Gaulle. In the 1960s, when France tried to subvert the dollar's role as the world's primary reserve currency, de Gaulle offered an alternative. He wanted to return the world to a reserve system based directly on gold bullion rather than on one major currency linked to gold. It was a naïve goal. The world economy by then had moved beyond the limitations set by a system tied to a finite supply of a precious metal. But de Gaulle understood that the dollar's unrivaled usage gave Americans what he would complain bitterly was an "exorbitant privilege." For a politician, the French president was unusually interested in global finance, and he knew that though the dollar pays no interest to its holders, the bill is a debt of the U.S.

government and its circulation overseas amounts to an interest-free loan to Washington.

The advantages to the American government, its corporations, and its citizens have expanded since the 1960s, and de Gaulle could hardly have imagined what the dollar's central role has bestowed. Most governments when pressed to raise money for domestic programs face a dilemma: raise taxes, cut back on those programs, or cut other programs, such as defense spending. None of these options is likely to win politicians votes. Countries can borrow money as a way to avoid that choice. But at best, it's usually a temporary solution. Typically, the more money governments borrow, the higher interest rates they must pay. Eventually it becomes prohibitively expensive for them to borrow further, and the costs of servicing the existing debt takes a toll on the economy.

The United States hasn't had to face this dilemma. Nor has it been penalized for borrowing ever-increasing amounts of money from foreign lenders. It's all part of a virtuous cycle that has been powering the global economy for the past ten years. Asian economies have kept their currencies cheap, making their goods inexpensive and boosting their sales to the United States. American consumers have responded by buying Asian products— cars, apparel, electronics, and so forth. In effect, Americans are sending their savings abroad. This creates a surplus of dollars in Asia that central banks there invest back into the United States through large purchases of Treasury and other U.S. bonds.

That starts the cycle all over again: keeping interest rates down and loans cheap for Americans, who can continue to borrow and spend. American companies can also borrow in the corporate bond market at cheap rates because their borrowing costs are priced off the low Treasury market yields. The overseas demand for dollars also enables Washington to run large deficits. If you exclude Social Security, Washington collects enough revenue to cover only about two-thirds of what it spends. That remaining third comes from foreign purchases of Treasury debt. The willingness of central banks to fund this budget gap means that U.S. politicians can avoid the classic tough choice between guns and butter. "The federal government, enjoying low funding costs, can have its cake and eat it too, boosting spending on both defense and social programs without having to resort to tax increases," Eichengreen wrote.

The concern is that this dynamic can't last indefinitely. And that when it ends, it could produce a violent unraveling. Once Nixon took the dollar off the gold standard, he paved the way for the American government to borrow vast sums of money that would never have been available to the United States when it backed its currency with bullion. This financial freedom to print more dollars and sell more Treasury bonds enabled the virtuous cycle to develop. But the market could still impose penalties on the dollar if it feels the United States has abused its privilege and has run itself too deeply into debt. Eventually, foreigners may become wary of owning so many dollars, funding America's record deficits and financing the superpower's huge debts (Europeans and others are starting to complain that foreign purchases of U.S. bonds help finance the American military activity that many foreigners oppose).

In 2005, U.S. interest payments on that foreign debt

topped the $100 billion mark for the first time—coming in at $114 billion, or about $310 million per day, according to Joseph Quinlan, Bank of America's chief market strategist. "That equates to slightly more than $1 million for each man, woman, and child in America—every day," Quinlan said. "The nation is addicted to foreign capital, or other people's money." And the rate at which the United States is going deeper into debt is accelerating: Those interest payments are more than double the amount the United States paid to its foreign creditors a decade ago.

Politicians are also taking up the cause of America's growing dependence on foreign debt. New York senator Hillary Clinton wrote a letter to Treasury Secretary Henry Paulson in February 2007 warning that such high levels of foreign obligations were a "source of great vulnerability" and that the U.S. economy "can easily be held hostage to the economic decisions being made in Beijing, Shanghai and Tokyo." Clinton is among the lawmakers to support bills in the House and Senate that call on the administration to take (unspecified) action when foreign ownership of Treasury debt reaches 25 percent of America's gross domestic product. Government data in March 2007 put foreign debt at around 16 percent of GDP.

Foreigners may also find that they can sell their products to their own, increasingly wealthy populations and that they no longer need to rely on cheap dollar exports. The reverse of global demand for the dollar and U.S. Treasury debt would turn the virtuous cycle inside out. As Eichengreen describes it, a falling dollar would put pressure on U.S. interest rates to rise. That, in turn, would make borrowing more expensive and slow economic growth. Stocks, bonds, and housing prices could also fall. Most Americans would no longer be able to spend beyond their means. "U.S. households, no longer living off of capital gains, will have to start saving again," Eichengreen wrote. "A significant decline in both consumption and investment will mean a recession in the United States."

Economists' biggest fear is of the damage a U.S. recession would inflict on the world economy. With the economies of Europe and Japan growing at slower rates, many exporters have come to rely on U.S. demand to sustain their businesses. That means a sudden U.S. slowdown or collapse in the dollar would threaten sales for companies around the world and could spark a global recession.

But it wouldn't take a dollar crisis to deal a blow to the global economy. Even a gradual reduction in the dollar's international use could have disruptive consequences. A one-currency world has helped unleash a period of unprecedented economic growth, fueled by a boom in cross-border trade and investment. The reasons are obvious: A single or dominant currency used internationally reduces transaction costs of converting one currency to another and thus spurs more trade and investment. That's why when Thailand trades with South Korea or Brazil, the transactions are usually carried out in dollars. A breakdown into currency blocs, even informal ones, would raise those transaction costs on exports, imports, travel and tourism, and cross-border investment. "Generally speaking, that would be the equivalent of instituting a global tax on almost everyone," Quinlan told me.

•   •   •

Near the end of Butler's public presentations on foreign currency accounts, there's one dramatic graph he
likes to flash on the screen for its startling effect. The
chart never fails to win some people over. It doesn't show
current account deficits or highlight central bank reserves
or international capital flows. It's a simple chart of the
dollar's performance since 1971, the year when the gold
standard ended and currency trading began. As the slide
illustrates, the dollar has experienced five extended trading cycles over this thirty-six-year period: a weakening
dollar from 1971 to 1978, a strengthening dollar from
1978 to 1985, dollar weakness again from 1985 to 1995,
dollar strength again from 1995 to 2002, and another period of weakening from 2002 to the present day.

It's immediately clear from the chart that the dollar
lost more ground during the weak years than it made
back during the strong ones. It was hit particularly hard
against the Japanese yen, Swiss franc, Deutsche mark,
and, later, the euro. Overall, since the dollar began trading in 1971, Butler calculated, it has lost 85 percent of its
value versus the major currencies. This chart helps him
hammer his main point home: If an investor had to
choose one currency in which to store his or her savings
since the time currencies began trading, the dollar would
not have been a very good choice.

Each of the dollar bear market periods has its own
unique circumstances. But Butler thinks in the long run
the dollar will continue falling because of simple supply
and demand. Without a gold standard, the United States

effectively can print as much new money as it wants. As the United States prints more dollars, it runs the risk that there will be a glut—that one day there will be more dollars than foreigners wish to hold. Maybe domination by one currency is just not meant to last for a superpower, Butler suggests, as governments can never avoid the temptation to debase their currency by printing more of it to avoid the tough choice of guns or butter.

As the world's first truly global currency, the dollar helped unleash a period of globalization never before seen, but it also changed the rules of the world economy in ways people are still trying to understand. It upended the relationships between states and created new opportunities—and new traps. Few would have guessed when Bretton Woods was signed in 1944 that Asian central banks would accumulate so many dollars they would gain a measure of power over the mighty U.S. economy. Or that a tiny, poor country like Ecuador could make the dollar its own currency. Or that the gold standard would falter and in its place would rise a $3-trillion-a-day foreign exchange market that would dwarf all other financial markets.

The average American may not have noticed it, but the dollar now appears to be gradually giving ground to other currencies. Washington can take steps to slow that process or, with bad policy decisions, it could accelerate it. But the government probably cannot stop it—not completely anyway, and not in a way that would return the world to a time when there was no euro and when China was an anticapitalist, inward-looking nation. As the dollar's grip over the world economy loosens, and

Americans find that some of their exorbitant privilege ebbs with it, they can at least take pride in this: There may never be another currency like the U.S. dollar, one so dominant and so readily accepted everywhere. It is a currency that somehow managed to transcend even the country of its origin. And just as the dollar's extraordinary rise in the twentieth century upended previous notions, the currency's reduced global role in this century is likely to change the rules of the world economy all over again.

BIBLIOGRAPHY

Chapter 1: **FISHING IN THE THREE-TRILLION-DOLLAR POND**

Kaufman, Michael T. *Soros: The Life and Times of a Messianic Billonaire*. New York: Alfred A. Knopf, 2002.

Chapter 2: **BLOWING UP THE MONEY FACTORY**

Altig, David E. *Why Is Stable Money Such a Big Deal?* Cleveland: Federal Reserve Bank of Cleveland, May 1, 2002.

Carlson, John B., and Benjamin D. Keen. *Where Is All the U.S. Currency Hiding?* Cleveland: Federal Reserve Bank of Cleveland, April 15, 1996.

Goodwin, Jason. *Greenback: The Almighty Dollar and the Invention of America*. New York: Picador, 2003.

Hershey, Robert D. "Treasury Says a Worker Took $1.7 Million in New $100 Bills." *New York Times*, 19 June 1994.

Jeter, Jon, and Brian Mooar. "Federal Worker Allegedly Stole Test Currency." *Washington Post*, 18 June 1994.

Lambert, Michael J., and Kristin D. Stanton. "Opportunities and Challenges of the U.S. Dollar as an Increasingly Global Currency: A Federal Reserve Perspective." *Federal Reserve Bulletin,* September 2001.

Mihm, Stephen. "No Ordinary Counterfeit." *New York Times Magazine,* 23 July 2006.

O'Brien, Dennis. "Former Engraving Employee Pleads Guilty to Stealing $1.6 Million in $100 Bills." *Baltimore Sun*, 7 October 1994.

Phillips, Michael M. "In Some Places, U.S. Money Isn't as Sound as a Dollar—Madagascar Likes Bills Signed by Snow; Rubin Series Trades at a Discount." *Wall Street Journal*, 2 November 2006.

Ramirez, Jr., Domingo. "Man Accused in $60,000 Theft." *Fort-Worth Star Telegram*, 22 April 2005.

Chapter 3: **MORE SOUND THAN THE POUND, AND GOOD AS GOLD**

Bordo, Michael D., Barry Eichengreen, and Douglas A. Irwin. "Is Globalization Today Really Different Than Globalization a Hundred Years Ago?" Working paper, National Bureau of Economic Research, Cambridge, Mass., 1999.

Broz, J. Lawrence. "Origins of the Federal Reserve System: International Incentives and the Domestic Free-rider Problem." *International Organization* 53, no. 1 (winter 1999).

Chernow, Ron. *The Death of the Banker: The Decline and Fall of the Great Financial Dynasties and the Triumph of the Small Investor.* New York: Vintage, 1997.

———. *The House of Morgan: An American Banking Dynasty and the Rise of Modern Finance.* New York: Atlantic Monthly Press, 1990.

———. *The Warburgs: The Twentieth-Century Odyssey of a Remarkable Jewish Family.* New York: Random House, 1993.

Eichengreen, Barry. "Sterling Past, Dollar's Future: Historical Perspectives on Reserve Currency Competition." Working paper, National Bureau of Economic Research, Cambridge, Mass., 2005.

———. "The Rise and Fall of a Barbarous Relic: The Role of Gold in the International Monetary System." Working paper, National Bureau of Economic Research, Cambridge, Mass., 1993.

Eichengreen, Barry, and Olivier Jeanne. "Currency Crisis and Unemployment: Sterling in 1931." Working paper, National Bureau of Economic Research, Cambridge, Mass., 1998.

Eichengreen, Barry, and Peter Temin. "The Gold Standard and the Great Depression." Working paper, National Bureau of Economic Research, Cambridge, Mass., 1997.

Gavin, Francis J., *Gold, Dollars, & Power: The Politics of International Monetary Relations, 1958–1971.* Chapel Hill: The University of North Carolina Press, 2006.

Jackson, Andrew. "Veto Message Regarding the Bank of the United States; July 10, 1832." The Avalon Project at Yale Law School. New Haven, Conn.

McKinnon, Ronald. "Trapped by the International Dollar Standard." *Journal of Policy Modeling* 27, no. 4 (June 2005): 477–485.

Treaster, Joseph B. *Paul Volcker: The Making of a Financial Legend.* Hoboken, N. J.: John Wiley & Sons, 2004.

World gross domestic product figures supplied by Global Financial Data in Los Angeles, Calif., www.globalfinancialdata.com.

Yergin, Daniel, and Joseph Stanislaw. *The Commanding Heights: The Battle Between Government and the Marketplace That Is Remaking the Modern World.* New York: Simon & Schuster, 1998.

Chapter 4: **THE TRIUMPHS AND TRAVAILS**
OF A DOLLAR COLONY

Beckerman, Paul, and Andres Solimano. *Crisis and Dollarization in Ecuador: Stability, Growth, and Social Equity.* Washington, D.C.: World Bank Publications, 2002.

Eichengreen, Barry, and Peter Temin, "The Gold Standard and the Great Depression." Working paper, National Bureau of Economic Research, Cambridge, Mass., 1997.

Luhnow, David. "Dollar Makes Its Case in Latin America." *Wall Street Journal,* 15 January 2001

Mosquera, Santiago. "Ecuadorian Government Submits 2008 Budget for Congressional Approval." *Global Insight,* September 2007.

Chapter 5: **THE DOLLAR'S BUYERS OF LAST RESORT**

Batson, Andrew. "China May Get More Daring With Its $1.07 Trillion Stash." *Wall Street Journal.* 15 February 2007.

Market News International, "China Gov. Econ Yu: China, Asia in Danger From Dollar Exposure," 12 December 2005.

Sesit, Michael R., and Craig Karmin. "How One Word Haunts the Dollar— Investors Tremble as Foreign Central Banks Speak of 'Diversification.' " *Wall Street Journal.* 17 March 2005.

Summers, Lawrence H. "America Overdrawn." *Foreign Policy,* no. 143 (July/August, 2004).

Chapter 6: **AN END TO AMERCIA'S EXORBITANT**
PRIVILEGE?

Eichengreen, Barry. "Sterling's Past, Dollar's Future: Historical Perspectives on Reserve Currency Competition." Working paper, National Bureau of Economic Research, Cambridge, Mass, 2005.

Juckes, Cheryl. "Ex-EU Commissioner Queries Euro's Future." *Reuters News,* 27 January 2006.

Kahn, Gabriel, and Marcus Walker. "Golden Handcuffs: With Italy in the Doldrums, Many Point Fingers at the Euro—Strong Currency Hurts Exports, Causing Some to Want Out." *Wall Street Journal,* 13 June 2005.

Lim, Ewe-Ghee. "The Euro's Challenge to the Dollar: Different Views from Economists and Evidence from COFER (Currency Composition of Foreign Exchange Reserves) and Other Data." Working paper no. 06/153, International Monetary Fund, Washington, D.C., 2006.

Samuelson, Robert J. "The Incredible Shrinking Dollar." *Newsweek,* 21 March 2005.

ACKNOWLEDGMENTS

Trying to explain the workings of the global economy through the lens of the dollar was never going to be an easy task. It was made more challenging still as the dollar's status evolved throughout the writing of this book. Making any sense of this required a good deal of help from several generous and intelligent people.

I am indebted to John Taylor and his staff at FX Concepts, who never complained when, upon returning from lunch or a coffee break, found me occupying their desk with notebook in hand. Nor did they object too strenuously when I pressed them to recall minute details of trades or events from days or weeks ago. Thanks also go to Larry Felix at the Bureau of Engraving and Printing, who was a gracious host with encyclopedic knowledge about currency.

This book owes much to Stanford professor Ronald McKinnon and Berkeley professor Barry Eichengreen, two of the foremost authorities on the role of currencies in the global financial system. Both were patient and charitable with their time, tutoring without ever forcing their views on me. My gratitude also goes to Heung Sik Choo at the Bank of Korea and Keehong Rhee at the

2

ACKNOWLEDGMENTS

253

Korean Investment Corporation for explaining their missions to me.

I'd like to thank all the Ecuadorians who shared details of their lives. A special debt goes to Clare St. Lawrence, my interpreter who translated as much about Ecuadorian culture as she did the Spanish language. Another thank you goes to Chuck Butler and his staff at EverBank.

At Crown Business publishing, I'm indebted to John Mahaney for believing in this book and working with me as the idea evolved. Thanks, too, to Lindsay Orman, who offered many good ideas of her own. I would never have a book without the support of my editors at *The Wall Street Journal,* who encouraged me to take on this project and granted me the time off to pursue it. Ken Wells and Roe D'Angelo were instrumental in helping me frame the subject and get it off the ground to begin with.

Finally, I'd like to thank my wife, Susanne, who endured my shifting moods and many weekends on her own, while I was anchored to my desk, trying to make deeper sense of how the buck operates in the modern world.

INDEX

About the Author

CRAIG KARMIN has been a reporter for the Money & Investing section of *The Wall Street Journal* since 1999, where he has covered international markets and foreign exchange. He has appeared on CNN and CNBC, and his work has also been published in *Barron's*, *The New Republic*, and *Newsweek International*. He lives in New York City with his wife and daughter.